FUZZY LOGIC

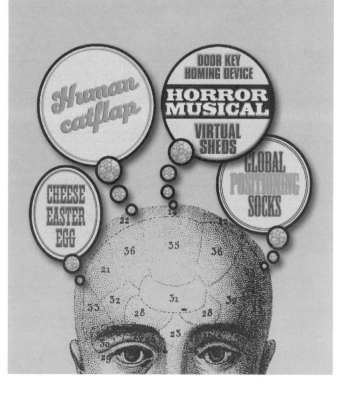

GREAT IDEAS DREAMT UP IN THE PUB

TOM WAINE

BOOKS

Published by the Campaign for Real Ale
230 Hatfield Road
St Albans
Hertfordshire AL1 4LW

www.camra.org.uk/books

ISBN: 978-1-85249-232-8

A CIP catalogue record for this book is available from the British Library

Printed in China

Head of Publications Joanna Copestick
Managing Editor Simon Hall
Project Editor Debbie Williams
Editor Leon Gray
Editorial Assistant Emma Lloyd
Design The Bridgewater Book Company Limited
Black and white illustrations Ivan Hissey
Colour plate illustrations Debbie Williams and Michael Whitehead
Marketing Manager Georgina Rudman

Picture Credits
38 Showface/Dreamstime.com; Debbie Williams; 39 Debbie Williams; 40 Don Chen/
Dreamstime.com; Mark Stout/Dreamstime.com; Gordon Ball/Dreamstime.com;
41 Paul Hickinbotham; 42 Norma Cornes/Dreamstime.com; Lucasz Witczak/Dreamstime.com;
Debbie Williams; 44 Max Blain/Dreamstime.com; Vincent Giordano//Dreamstime.com; Lucian
Coman/Dreamstime.com; Pavel Losevsky/Dreamstime.com; Tihis/Dreamstime.com; 45 Mandy
Godbehear/Dreamstime.com; Debbie Williams; Arnaud Messager; Tomasz Trojanowski/
Dreamstime.com; 46 Cora Reed/Dreamstime.com; Debbie Williams; Ron Chapple/
Dreamstime.com; Robert Young/Dreamstime.com; 47 Emma Lloyd; Debbie Williams;
48 Ene/Dreamstime.com; Tomasz Trojanowski/Dreamstime.com; Lyn Baxter/Dreamstime.com;
Milan Kopcock/Dreamstime.com; Kati Neudert/Dreamstime.com; Kuzma/Dreamstime.com;
Millan/Dreamstime.com; Cecilia Lim/Dreamstime.com; 49 Debbie Williams; www.bigphoto.com;
50 Eric Isselée/Dreamstime.com; Pawel Strykowski/Dreamstime.com; Jacek Chabraszewski/
Dreamstime.com; James Steidl/Dreamstime.com; Gene Lee/Dreamstime.com; Debbie Williams;
51 Guyerwood/Dreamstime.com; Rick Lord/Dreamstime.com; Jesse/Dreamstime.com;
David Gaylor/Dreamstime.com; 52 Feng Yu/Dreamstime.com; Steven Pepple/Dreamstime.com;
Costea Amar Adrian/Dreamstime.com

CONTENTS

Introduction   6

Pub Technology   8

Art & Media Darlings   14

Men are from Bars and
Women are from Venus   20

Food   28

Medical Matters   32

Communications   38

Personal Grooming   46

Sport & Leisure   52

Miscellaneous Madness   62

Pub Theories   70

Full-colour Ideas   77

Readers' Fuzz   93

INTRODUCTION

Ever since there were pubs, people have talked a load of nonsense in them. Every day of every week, drunken geniuses across the land sit in the comfort of their local boozer, dreaming up schemes to make a quick buck. Marketing professionals 'think outside of the box', management consultants come up with 'blue-sky ideas', but most of us eventually realize that it's complete and utter rubbish. Public-house revelations occasionally touch on brilliance (the DNA double helix, for example), but for the most part alcohol-fuelled ideas are just plain old tosh. This sobering notion does little to dissuade your average pub mastermind, however, who is both encouraged and deluded with every pint. The next morning, what was destined to set the world alight and change the course of human evolution dissolves as quickly as an Alka-Seltzer, gulped down before an impending trip to IKEA.

Pub ideas can be benign, surreal and even vaguely plausible. They span many different subject areas, all of which provide us with a fascinating insight into the mind of the pub genius. Over the years, I've been extremely fortunate to witness some truly magnificent nonsense in pubs all around the country — inebriated prophesies passionately discussed by both friends and complete strangers alike. I've even seen the most stoic, hardened commuter reduced to tears of hysterical laughter at the thought of one of these ideas actually bearing the fruits of its drunken labour. In this collection, I've included some of the very best ideas that grew out of pub discussion, and I invite you to take them all in — on the train or in the toilet, at bedtime or perhaps even over a few pints down at your local pub. I would also love to hear your own ideas — please visit www.pubideas.com.

I'll now set about trying to capture the essence of fuzzy logic, as well as shamelessly plugging the think tanks (pubs/bars) and stimulants (booze) that enabled these wonderful ideas to take flight.

RULES

First off, I need to establish the few ground rules to establish what exactly constitutes a valid pub idea:

- It should be a series of thoughts or ideas that for the most part are only considered to be genius after a few pints within the four walls of your local hostelry.
- It should receive nothing more than a frown from your bank manager.
- It should be no more likely to come to fruition than the England football team winning the World Cup.
- Marketing professionals and advertisers are excluded. Whether created in a pub or not, you people make a living out of this sort of crap.

PubTechnology

On February 28, 1953, the biologist Francis Crick swaggered into the Eagle public house in Cambridge and announced: 'We've discovered the secret of life.' He was, of course, referring to his discovery of the DNA double helix, along with the American James Watson. Unfortunately the only similarity between this Nobel Prize-winning revelation and the collection of scientific gems in this chapter is that they all took place in the pub.

SEE FULL-COLOUR IDEAS 2 AND 3

GPS – GLOBAL POSITIONING SOCKS

One angry punter sat in a pub in Brighton incensed by the mysterious disappearance of yet another sock. A table of sympathetic friends set to work on the problem. One pint of Old Speckled Hen and a couple of glasses of wine later, one of the group happened upon an idea so huge that we all sat in silence for what seemed like an eternity:

'Satellite navigation socks,' she repeated. 'Use some high-tech computer software to track the whereabouts of your socks 24 hours a day.'

Then last orders rang and the idea disappeared without trace like a sock in the washing machine of life.

When approached, a leading NASA scientist thought that the idea was great but that the cost of the software would be prohibitive (approximately £3,599 per sock).

Formula
(Old Speckled Hen[1])+(Glass of Wine)

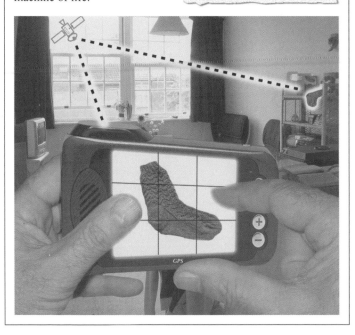

VIRTUAL SHEDS

See full-colour idea 2

A friend of mine, Jim, lives in a block of flats in Battersea. One Sunday afternoon we were chatting over a couple of fine ales in his local, The Prince Arthur. Around the two-pint mark, Jim surrendered this little beauty:

'What I need is a virtual shed! A shed for people like me who live in flats. You could fill it with the usual crap – broken mower, dusty deckchair, that kind of thing.'

He continued:

'You could buy a virtual-reality helmet and gloves. Use the software to specify your shed requirements, pop on the helmet and gloves and away you go. You could even upgrade to an allotment with shed included!'

Then you could spend all weekend:

◆ **Trying to remember the code for the padlock on the shed door.**

◆ **Tidying the shed.**

◆ **Creosoting the shed to cover up the graffiti.**

◆ **Dispersing drunken teenagers.**

◆ **Dealing with pests.***

◆ **Weeding the allotment (use the software to specify how much spare time you have on your hands).***

◆ **Sabotaging next door's allotment (vegetable rage).***

Only available with allotment upgrade.

After further discussion and some quick calculations of development costs, Jim eventually withdrew the idea, concluding that it might actually be cheaper to get an allotment and put a real shed on it.

DOOR KEY HOMING DEVICE

'You try and negotiate the front door lock late at night, while drunk and relying on stealth and double vision alone. Even to someone who ordinarily has amazing coordination, it's a tricky prospect and not something that improves with training. The conditions required for each door-unlocking are unique and can make the job insurmountable – adverse weather conditions, the amount and type of alcohol consumed and other factors such as the double lock, for example.'

When the Williams' front door began to resemble a dartboard at the Lakeside darts tournament, they thought they had finally struck gold with the following pub idea:

The **Door Key Homing Device** relies on two infrared sensors – one on the key fob and another built in to your front door. When the two sensors align, they emit a succession of beeps. The further away the key is from the door, the longer the interval between beeps. But the closer you get to the lock, the shorter and faster the sound. When you hear a loud continuous BEEEEEEP! you know you're locked onto the target.

NowScientist

HUMAN CAT FLAP IDEA NO LONGER OUT IN THE COLD

Can't find your keys anywhere? Locked out again? Walked home on all fours after a skinful?

These were some of the questions from a scientific study conducted five years ago by a team of City College students. The results of the study were conclusive:

'More than 80 per cent of the public answered "yes" to one of the survey questions. As a result of these findings, we were compelled to find a solution,' said a spokesperson for the college.

Students from the London-based college then embarked on several years of extensive research. The breakthrough came last year, when one of the researchers picked up a magazine in his local pub: 'I saw an advert for a cat flap, and it all clicked into place. We just needed to apply the same technology,' he said.

Soon after, the first prototype was built and tested in the college labs, but it courted controversy among the other faculties:

'No one understood the significance of our work,' explained one of the team.

Despite this early cynicism, the students drank a lot in preparation. As testing gathered momentum, all the hard work paid off:

'Finally, we had a workable prototype.'

The human cat flap works using a uniquely coded magnetic collar, which allows only the person wearing it to enter the house. This eliminates the problem of unwanted strays. The four-way security locking system ensures that once you get home, you stay home… at least until you're sober enough to work out how to open the front door with a key.

The students later developed the Automatic Junk Food feeder based on the same technology as the flap. Fill up the feeder before you go out, and the lid pops open automatically as soon as you get home. The team also developed a handy optional reservoir attachment, providing over a gallon of thirst-quenching, hangover-preventing tea.

'The results have been staggering,' said one university lecturer. 'For many years we've been faced with the same problem, and now it has been solved thanks to the good work of some of our top students.'

See full-colour idea 3

30 SECONDS

Saturday night navigation system

An off-the-shelf solution to get you home safely on a Saturday night. As beer levels dull the cerebral cortex, the GPS navigation system takes control. Simply enter the coordinates of the pub before you leave home, and the GPS technology does the rest. Each system comes complete with a headset, voice-recognition software and speech synthesizer to guarantee you safe passage to your door.

Extra RAM – for people over 30

Do you find new technology mind-boggling? Do you struggle to remember where you left your car keys? Or are you too slow to respond to your work colleague's callous put-downs? Then it's time to add some extra RAM. Due to hit the shops in the run-up to Christmas, this revolutionary chip implant for memory-challenged thirty-somethings will come with a DIY installation guide.

Take to bed toilet

Savour the reassuring coolness of porcelain from the comfort of your own bed and be sure of a good night's sleep with Dr Armitage's Take To Bed Toilet Technology.

ART&MEDIA DARLINGS

While the arts and media take centre stage in our modern world, it's all a bit of a mixed bag. Flick through the channels on your remote and endure the horrors of real life on the 24-hour news networks, or savour the psychological drama played out on the latest reality TV shows. Stroll through the London galleries and marvel at Rembrandt's butchery with a brush, or admire the intricate saw strokes inherent in the art of Damien Hirst. All this begs the question… what is art? What makes good media? I'm not even going to attempt to provide an answer within the confines of this book. Let's just accept that the arts and media are purely subjective. With this in mind, I think it's now safe to proffer the following pub-based art and media 'darlings'.

SEE FULL-COLOUR IDEAS 4 AND 5

DIY TURNER PRIZE STARTER KIT

The Turner Prize is an annual award bestowed to the best British artist under the age of 50. Judged by a panel of respected art aficionados, the £25,000 prize is presented to the winner during an alcohol-fuelled ceremony at Tate Britain, where an exhibition of the short-listed artists is on display several months before the winner is announced.

Following a pub discussion of Martin Creed's 'Lights Going On and Off' installation, which swept the 2001 Turner Prize, there followed this snapshot of artistic genius:

THE DIY TURNER PRIZE STARTER KIT

The kit contains a short passage of predetermined indecipherable bullshit that can be loosely applied to a random box of items. A typical starter kit might include:

1 x predetermined bullshit
1 box
1 turnip

1 band saw
1 rubber washer
2 screws from some flat-pack furniture
some paint

How this is linked together is left to the discretion of the purchaser. Even with a price tag of £25, which includes automatic entry into the competition, the wannabe artist could stand a very real chance of winning, given the past form.

I approached a spokesperson for the Turner Prize with our idea, but they refused to comment on this initiative, dismissing it all as 'a load of nonsense'.

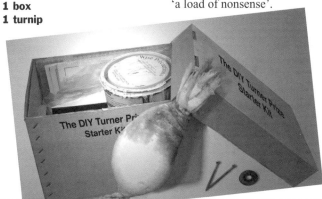

BIG BROTHER / 1984

Disillusioned with the current obsession with reality TV shows, Gus came up with the ultimate reality format over a few pints of Skullsplitter in his local one Friday night:

'Everyone who avoids the spectacle of Friday-night live TV eviction by going to the pub instead nominates 12 of the country's most annoying celebrities to spend 18 weeks in the house.'

Celebrity candidates for selection include, among others (the list goes on and on):

◆ **Those who measure their success by the amount of column inches they attract.**
◆ **Those made famous by dating a Premiership footballer.**
◆ **Those famous for turning up to award ceremonies to open the envelopes.**
◆ **Those who found fame by falling out of their dress.**

The select few are rounded up and installed in the house for 18 weeks, cheered in by a fake audience of jobbing actors and not-so-lookalikes. Everything seems normal – the celebrity housemates are forced to perform an endless list of degrading and shameless tasks. But here's the twist… No one is actually watching. No one even knows about the show. Each week, the producer evicts the least offensive celebrity. Kicked out into an empty car park, the only thing to greet them is a minicab to take them home (providing that they have the fare, of course). The last remaining, and therefore most appalling, celebrity would be imprisoned for the full term, providing TV viewers with 18 weeks of irritation-free bliss. The best part is filming each celebrity's reaction to the show – it's another reality TV programme in its own right!

THE HORROR MUSICAL

'Most musicals are horrors, but that's not what I meant.'

'Go on,' I said. Paul didn't need any encouragement.

'Well, I've been subjected to musicals ever since I was a kid. Some were mildly entertaining, some were absurd, most were diabolical. So what do you think about the world's first horror musical?'

'I still don't understand,' I replied.

'Well, it's called **A Nightmare on 42nd Street**, with an all-singing, all-dancing Freddy Krueger character. Each member of the cast starts to sing a hit song from a West End musical. During their performance, Freddy inflicts upon them the most unimaginable pain and they die. As the curtain falls in record

time, the audience is then treated to the untimely death of Andrew Lloyd Webber. Surely this would strike a cord with anyone who's ever been forced to sit through a performance because their partner told them to?' With the carefully structured plot set in stone, I endeavoured to find Paul his West End contact. I called all the leading theatrical agents in London, but I've still not found a producer who's willing to take on Paul's project.

OKAY KARAOKE

See full-colour idea 4

Karaoke has long been a divisive fixture in pubs. This pair of ideas from a pub-goer called Duncan attempts to reinstate the serenity of the pub environment without spoiling the dreams of stardom-seeking pub singers.

Idea one came at 9:30pm on Friday night following two pints of Fursty Ferret:

Quiet Karaoke

Inspired by the fashionable 'quiet parties' of London's artistic fraternity, Quiet Karaoke would involve encasing performers in a soundproof perspex booth. Headsets would then be provided to anyone in the pub tone-deaf enough to listen. If a performer was singing unbearably, punters could simply remove their headphones and, with a bit of luck, the would-be crooner would get the message and relent.

10:30pm. Idea two:
'No – even better...' said Duncan, a good hour later and with a pint of Bishop's Finger to steel his confidence, '...how about this:'

Trapdoor Karaoke

The aspiring singer wails out loud for the whole pub to hear. Each punter in the pub is armed with a remote control device for voting.

There are two choices: 'Stay' and 'Go Now'. If the majority of the pub press 'Go Now', then the singer disappears through a trapdoor and is jettisoned into a legally binding record contract with a high-trouser-wearing millionaire record-label manager.

THE NON-CELEBRITY MAGAZINE

Here's some fuzzy logic dreamt up in a doctor's surgery waiting room and later discussed down the pub. The idea came from someone with little interest in reading about the homes, gardens or weddings of the rich and famous. When faced with a waiting room filled only with this type of vacuous literature, she was forced to think up alternative possibilities to cope with the lengthy wait to see a GP.

'I'd rather see a magazine with similar content gossiping about the general public than about these so-called celebrities. This would make for a far more compelling read.'

Please refer to full-colour idea 5 for more details.

RADIO CRIMES

PICK OF THE WEEK

Reality

Dosh in the Attic
Monday 11.00pm BBC10
Two bent coppers raid more homes in and around London in the search for hidden treasures. Last week, John from Chingford was looking to raise £120,000 for a holiday apartment in Florida. And John's dreams of a second home came true when the two PCs discovered a kilo of cocaine in his attic. Will they have the same success this week?

The Y? Factor
Saturday 5.00pm ITV
It's hard to believe that there can still be any undiscovered pub singers out there. But with a record-breaking 10 applications for the second series, judges Simon Trowell, Sharon Osburn and Louis Welsh are confident they can find Britain's next crooner. The first show in the series focuses on the auditions conducted in and around Swindon.

Sport

Club Swap
Thursday 10.00pm BBC12
Follow the plight of the Premiership team you voted to swap with ill-fated United of the third division. Each team keeps their goalie, central defender, central midfielder, and top scorer, but for the rest of the squad it's a straight swap!

The World Fruit Machine Finals from Blackpool
Sunday 11.30pm ITV9
Six-times loser Sean 'Hold The Bells, Should Come In' Smith attempts to win this annual event for the first time. Five finalists battle it out on different machines, with only their giros and forty cigarettes at stake, to win enough tokens for the coveted china dog trophy in the window.

Pro/Celebrity Golf Night
Monday 12.05am SKY SPORTS 25
Highlights of this weekend's golfing action, as the pros and celebrities fumble their way around a moonlit St Andrews. We apologise if most viewers are unable to see any balls.

The Admiral's Fag
Wednesday 12.45am Channel 45
Highlights of this year's cross-channel cigarette-smuggling race.

Food

Ready Steady Crook
Tuesday 4.30pm ITV21
Last in the current series. The celebrity chefs help the inmates bake an exploding surprise for the governor at HMP Strangeways.

Lifestyle

Changing Rooms
Friday 11.00am CHANNEL 5.5
Webcam footage brought to you live from the changing rooms at Topshop in Oxford Street.

Wildlife

Lion's Den
Thursday 9.00pm NATIONAL
Five Millwall season-ticket holders are given £250,000 to invest in this season's new signings. This week, transfer hopefuls state their claim to a contract in front of the panel of devoted fans. Humiliation, intimidation and strong language guaranteed.

Survival Special
Sunday 8.00pm NATIONAL 2
With only one credit card to his name, this worldly American shows Ray Ears how to survive in a shopping mall for an entire weekend.

Gameshow

Death or No Death
Sunday 7.00pm Channel 405
22 boxes, one life and 21 gruesome executions – another deposed despot gambles with his life. Presented as usual by a goateed millionaire.

MEN ARE FROM BARS AND WOMEN ARE FROM VENUS

A relationship is just about the most difficult test in a person's life. It requires an incredible amount of work and a range of life skills: kindness, compromise, forgiveness and sexual prowess… the list goes on and on. Relationship experts devote their lives to trying to teach us these vital skills, unselfishly making a fortune in the process. So it may come as no surprise that failure to understand and appreciate the differences between the sexes accounts for about half of all beer-fuelled pub discussion. Night after night, scorned partners find themselves embroiled in more impromptu pub counselling, resulting in the sort of revelatory improvements, ideas and theories outlined in this chapter.

SEE FULL-COLOUR IDEAS 6 AND 7

PARENT CRÈCHE

See full-colour idea 6

One Friday night on the way home from work, I sat down next to a stressed-out, suited gent who was downing a can of Wadworth 6x. Steve worked for a City law firm and looked like he had the weight of the world on his pinstriped shoulders. We got chatting. A few cans later, he told me his troubles… a trip to IKEA the following day. Steve didn't have a problem with IKEA; rather his midday trip clashed with his Premiership team's kick-off. Steve confessed that he'd used up all his football credits. He'd already watched two games that week.

Formula

Midweek televised = Trip to
football?   IKEA

OK, the forward-thinking furniture giant has already set up a crèche for the kids. But what about the parents?

'A parent crèche is a great idea,' Steve enthused. 'All you'd need to do is hand over your credit card to the other half so she can shop in bliss. Meanwhile, you relax in a bar with Sky Sports and a choice of newspapers, comfy slippers and a range of the latest XBOX games.'

I never saw Steve again. I checked the football scores, though. His team lost 3–2.

CARD MESSAGE GENERATOR

One particular pub genius landed himself in trouble when his girlfriend criticised his unimaginative birthday card greetings. He came up with the solution over a few pints of Whistle Belly Vengeance – his favourite tipple:

'What I need is a card message generator. Just type in the recipient's name and age, the occasion, my relationship to the recipient and how strongly I feel about them. Then out pops my heartfelt message of congratulations/condolence. I'd need a new, sincere and original message each time, so there's no risk of repeating myself.'

Card Message Generator can generate a range of useful templates:

Wedding anniversaries – guarantees the correct names and anniversary date, first song at wedding, the weather on the day

How and when we first met – how, when, where, amount drunk (optional)

Mother's Day cards – includes in-law expansion pack (extra cost)

Newborn baby cards – remembers the name, time of birth, weight, etc…

THE LOO LECTERN

One night down the pub, Helen revealed that her boyfriend had taken to using the loo as a reading room. Every Sunday morning, he would barricade himself in the toilet with enough reading material to see most people through a two-week holiday. A quick survey of the surrounding tables revealed that this was a common problem, and there seemed to be a higher percentage of male toilet scholars than female ones. Helen found the whole idea both repulsive and unhygienic. Several pints later, her solution was forthcoming:

'What my boyfriend needs is a loo lectern – a fold-out, sterile stand to hold the reading material away from the toilet. Now I just need to find a way of wiring up the toilet seat to the mains. 240 volts passing through his arse and I'm sure he'd get the message.'

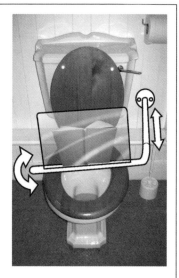

BATH BOOKS

Ever dropped your book in the bath? Attempted to turn the pages with your nose to prevent them from getting wet? Books and magazines should be published in laminated format for bath-time reading sessions. Our Bath Books discussion came shortly after talk of the Loo Lectern had ended, but a disgruntled male toilet scholar did not approve:

'Why not put an extra cold tap outside the bathroom so our bath bookworm would know when someone was waiting to use the loo.'

We all decided that it probably wasn't a good idea to wire the bathtub up to the mains.

PERFUMED PANTS

One night, I overheard two girls talking about their respective partners' bodily emissions. The bottom line was this:

'My Jack often comes home with a belly-full of beer and curry/kebab after a night out with the lads. While I still find him adorable as he snuggles up to me in a drunken stupor, his bodily emissions are anything but desirable. I would LOVE to find him some perfumed pants… you know, fitted with a sweet-smelling scratch patch on the back or something. Then he can scratch his arse as much as he likes.'

DATE-BREAKING SERVICE

As I sat in a bar, my friend recalled the horrors of a recent blind date. It had been a disastrous evening, and she'd struggled to get away. Her date just didn't get the message.

'What would be really useful,' she began, *'would be a number that I could discreetly call or text the next time I get into trouble. They could terminate the date within an hour of my call.'*

'How would they do that?' I asked.

My friend then enlisted the help of some girls at a nearby table. After a few drinks, they came up with the date-breaking service. The service provides tiered levels of membership depending on how rich or desperate you are.

- **Bronze** One text or phone call pretending to be a family member in distress.
- **Silver** Text messages sent at timed intervals culminating in an angry message from a jealous ex-boyfriend/girlfriend.
- **Gold** Specially trained staff evacuate you from your nightmare.
- **Platinum** Premium membership for serial blind-daters.

BIRD'S-EYE MAP OF BRITAIN

A frosty-looking couple sat in a Yorkshire pub one Saturday evening. The couple sat in silence for about an hour, finished their food and then left. Shortly afterwards, the landlord came over to the table, collected their glasses and informed us that the couple had fallen out over the woman's map-reading skills. As I chuckled, Jo shot me an ice-cold stare. Days before, we'd been in exactly the same situation.

Our newly appointed map-idea steering group – the landlord, his wife, Jo, myself, and a retired sheepdog called Bess – then sat down over a few pints of Tetley's to discuss the map-reading ability of the sexes.

This is a map of Britain from a woman's perspective, including the following:

◆ POP-UP INDICATORS for those who don't know their loft from their right.

◆ HANDY POUCH for spare eye make-up and mirror.

◆ USEFUL PHRASES to use in the event of a dispute: 'Well, you obviously weren't paying attention when I told you to turn left...'

◆ SCALED MAP to include specific places of interest: shoe shops, hair salons, that kind of thing.

◆ SCENIC-ROUTE FINDER to use in the event of a dispute: 'Yes, I'm sure I wanted to go this way. Look at the scenery. Isn't it lovely?'

SYNTHETIC FEET

ONE PAIR OF SYNTHETIC, MICROWAVEABLE FEET FOR SALE

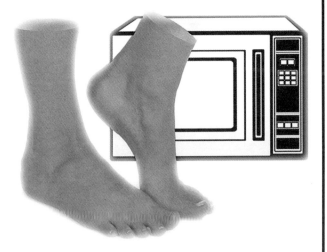

Ideal if your partner likes to put their cold feet on yours in bed at night. Heat the feet in the microwave and slip them into bed.

Customizable corns, calluses and verrucas for guaranteed authenticity.

Microwave takes approxiately 2 minutes

THE
AIR FRESHENER
TOOTH

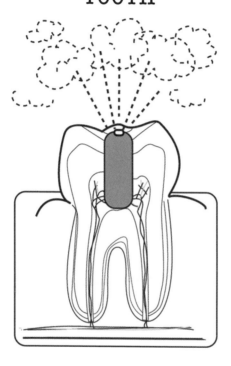

Morning breath doesn't discriminate: it happens to us all, whether you're Brad Pitt, Angelina Jolie or Keith Chegwin. Now everyone can benefit from the very latest cutting-edge tooth-freshening technology.

Easy to fit yourself or ask your dentist to fit it for you.

The Air Freshener Tooth keeps your mouth fresh 24 hours a day. Replace every six months for a new aroma.

Available in sandalwood, fruits of the forest, spearmint and overpowering lavender.

FOOD

British people, or 'Roast Beefs' as we are known by the French, have long been chastised for a perceived lack of culinary creativity. I've always felt this to be a little unfair, so I took to the pubs of Britain to test the French hypothesis. Looking up at the menus on the chalkboards revealed a host of national treasures: Chicken Tikka Masala, Lasagne and Chips and Chilli con Carne, to name but a few. In light of this gastronomic revolution, I invited some of the worst 'food-phobic' British pub-goers to talk about their food. The resulting food-related pub chat can only restore a sense of British national pride.

SEE FULL-COLOUR IDEA 8

Alternative EASTER EGGS

Easter eggs are a seasonal treat for all the family. Kids' eyes widen in awe as they wander down the Easter-egg aisles of the local supermarket, and it's a well-known fact that women prefer chocolate to many other vital activities. After a few pints of Old Mottled Cock – the guest ale down at their local – a consortium of savoury-toothed activists came up with the following alternatives to the traditional chocolate Easter egg.

THE CHEESTER EGG

'Easter egg companies need to wake up,' remarked Andy. 'For millions of us without a sweet tooth, cheese is our chocolate. There's a potential gold mine out there.'

'How about a range of Cheester Eggs of varying sizes?' Andy continued. 'The egg could be encased in the same plethora of packaging as a traditional chocolate egg, but it would be made entirely of cheese. Inside each egg will be different mini-cheeses and, of course, some crackers. Maybe even a small bottle of port or a jar of pickle on the inside?'

I contacted a leading chocolate egg manufacturer about the potential of the Cheester Egg, but they failed to see the enormous possibilities of this pub idea.

'Although we can see the potential of your savoury egg, we have no plans to venture into this market at this time.'

Chocolate eggs beware – there might be a new type of egg in town.

THE SCOTCH EASTER EGG

North of the border, the controversial alternative to the traditional Easter egg is the Scotch Easter Egg. If you've never tasted this Scottish delicacy, you're in for a treat. It's a sublime fusion of sausage meat and cold,

MATURE

WENSLEYDALE

· ORGANIC ·

A PERFECTLY SPUN
EGG OF OUR BEST EVER
WENSLEYDALE CHEESE

hard-boiled egg, coated in breadcrumbs and deep-fried – a wonderfully fattening orb of artery-clogging goodness, and the most obvious contender to replace the conventional chocolate egg. Just head down to your local newsagents.

'For the Easter version to be viable, the standard hen's egg should be replaced by a larger version,' Lisa explained. 'Until the Easter-egg manufacturers wake up to the growing needs of the savoury-savvy market, we should provide the public with a recipe. You just can't beat the look, feel and sentiment of a home-made savoury egg.'

It was futile arguing with Lisa and her passion for the Scotch Easter Egg, so here it is:

Ingredients
Makes one Scotch Egg
1 hard-boiled ostrich egg, well chilled

1.5 lb pork sausage meat
2 large hen's eggs, well beaten
½ cup flour
¾ cup fine breadcrumbs
vegetable oil for frying

Turn on your fat fryer. If you are using a hob or stove, pour enough oil into a pan. Heat the oil slowly so it doesn't spatter – gradually increase the temperature to 350°F (175°C).

Roll the ostrich egg in flour. Carefully coat it with a thick layer of the sausage meat. Tightly pack the mixture around the egg – there should be no white showing. Brush the surface with the beaten eggs and then roll it in breadcrumbs until it's completely covered.

Deep fry for approximately 8–10 minutes. When the egg is ready, it will be golden brown and the sausage will be cooked all the way through. Refrigerate for a couple of hours and then serve cold in the traditional fashion.

RESTAURANTS 23 R

PREGNANT PIZZA

BIZARRE toppings delivered straight to your door!

24-HOUR SERVICE

Try our Classico Supreme pizza:
Raw pasta, tuna, mayonnaise,
coal, chalk and whipped cream
Free delivery – we know
it's difficult to get up

High St, Bedford
Tel: 01632 555 0147

Déjà Vu Kebab – Been here before?
25 High Street . . . . .Tel 01632 555 0144
Cod Alone Knows – Might be fish and chips
26 High Street . . . . .Tel 01632 555 0177
Ring Of Fire – Indian restaurant
27 High Street . . . . .Tel 01632 555 5550

PAVLOV'S BURGERS

Wait for the bell at your local and then come
on down for an unsupervised fight in the
queue followed by a cheap, forgettable meal.

High St, Croydon
Tel: 01632 555 0774

CHINESE LOTTERY
TAKEAWAY

 IT COULD BE YOURS!
Select six numbers and see what
turns up on your doorstep.

*Or try our Lucky Dip meal, with
FREE fortune cookie.*
Specialists in charismatic duck.
High St, Blackpool
Tel: 01632 555 0174

The UK's First Cake Gym
A revolution in fitness!

Come in for a trial today:
Choose your preferred cake. Your workout time is then calculated for you by one
of our slightly overweight instructors. Sit on an exercise bike, watch telly, chat to
some friends and burn off the calorific value while you eat.

Gymnasium with latest cakevascular equipment
◆ **The latest non-resistance technology**
◆ **Beautiful relaxing changing suites with complimentary scones**
◆ **Large aerobic studio equipped with food vending machines**
◆ **Free Solero**

Classes available:
◆ **Black Forest Body Pump**
◆ **L.B.T** (Lemon cake, Battenberg and Teacake)
◆ **Body Combat** (Cake fighting)
◆ **Yogart**
◆ **Spin**
◆ **Aqua Fat**

CAKEFIRST FITNESS
TEL 01632 555 0156

MEDICAL MATTERS

Advances in modern medicine and society's obsession with dieting, fitness plans and holistic therapies have all contributed to improving the health and longevity of the nation. Even the pub is receiving its own government-induced enema, flushing the most hardened smokers from its hallowed carpets and nicotine-stained walls. It's not only the atmosphere that's changing in pubs. It's the conversation. As I was researching this book, I noticed a sharp increase in the discussion of medical matters. Some of the best medical pub ideas are gathered here for your consideration. You'll be glad to know that most are still reassuringly unhealthy.

SEE FULL-COLOUR IDEAS 9, 10 AND 11

DESIGNER CATHETERS

See full-colour idea 9

The designer catheter was born out of a friend's torturous *Lord of the Rings* cinema experience. What he saw of the film was magnificent, but its length, coupled with the pints he had drunk beforehand, made the evening extremely harrowing.

At an epic 178 minutes, the film required no less than four toilet stops. He could have gone again but decided to sit it out, sensing the tension building up in the people around him. The cinema catheter was his solution.

'With hindsight, some sort of cinema catheter would have been the ideal solution. A series of tubes could be stitched into the lining of some specially adapted trousers and connected to a pouch that looks a bit like a bum bag. Then you could just sit back, wee at will and enjoy the film, tutting at other cinemagoers as they edge past you on their way to the toilet.'

The obvious question came out: 'Are you taking the piss?' But after careful consideration, I suggested that it might be better to drink a bit less before going to see a film.

Formula
Film length = Number of drinks
Seat location   to safely consume

This particular pub genius has gone on to bigger and better things. Whenever we meet up for a few pints, he tells me of his latest additions to the designer catheter range.

Festival catheter
Designed with the weekend music festival in mind, this particular catheter ensures you'll keep your place in the mosh pit and avoid unpleasant encounters with a well-used Portaloo. The festival catheter accessorizes the original cinema concept with a large rucksack and trousers lined with urine-filled tubes.

Train catheter
An essential travel companion on rail networks where the conductor has locked the doors of the toilet cubicles on packed commuter trains.

MAGIC SPONGE

While viewing a Premiership football match on TV over a few pints one day, the boss of a telesales company could not believe the amazing rejuvenating properties of the sponge and spray used to treat the injured players.

One player fell to the ground, writhing in apparent agony, following a typically innocuous challenge. On came the physio, armed with what appeared to be a sponge and a spray can. Within twenty seconds of the magic treatment, the player got up and started running around like a cheetah on cocaine.

'Amazing,' she said. 'If I could get hold of one of those sponges and cans of spray, I could cut absenteeism at work by 100 per cent. When someone phones in sick on a Monday morning, I could just drop by their house, administer the magic sponge and spray can and render them fit for work with more vigour than before the weekend.'

I contacted several Premiership clubs the following week to find out the name of the spray and to see whether the sponge could be safely used at work. So far they have all declined to comment.

ANTACID COCKTAIL

The fusion techniques employed by cocktail barmen, or mixologists as they now like to be called, have so far failed to examine the untapped market of the indigestion-suffering general public, according to our next pub theorist. Blighted by acid indigestion, she came up with this suggestion.

The antacid cocktail is made in the same way as a normal cocktail. Plenty of crushing, shaking and unnecessary bottle juggling, but with the helpful addition of a soothing antacid to buffer the acidity of the spirits and citrus fruits. This idea gave rise to the following cocktail suggestions:

- ◆ **A Slippery Tipple**
- ◆ **Singapore Seltzer**
- ◆ **Long Island Iced Tums**
- ◆ **The Sloe Comfortable Walk**
- ◆ **Home From the Pub**

HYPOCHONDRIAC TEXT SERVICE

See full-colour idea 10

According to someone I spoke to in a pub in London one evening, it takes a lot of discipline and effort to be a hypochondriac. This next pub idea came about to help busy professionals maintain a healthy interest in all unhealthy medical matters.

'If you don't have time to keep abreast of the latest illnesses, what about a hypochondriac text service? Text the words "I'm ill" to the given number, and for 25 pence you'll receive the most up to date illnesses, complete with symptoms. Each text should start with the words "I don't want to worry you, but..."'

GROW YOUR OWN ORGAN ON A MOUSE

See full-colour idea 11

With the NHS in a state of flux and transplant waiting lists at an all-time high, Paul's solution to the problem of organ donation rendered his rowdy audience of pub-goers speechless:

'You know those grow-your-own kits that kids get to put on their windowsill at home? How about a grow-your-own-organ-on-a-mouse kit? You saw that mouse, right? The one with the ear? You could pick one up from the local science shop and then add the right solution, depending on which organ you wish to grow. When the organ reaches the right size, donate it to the NHS.'

The stunned landlord broke the stunned silence by suggesting that perhaps Paul's brain was growing on a mouse somewhere!

DESIGNER INJURIES

Beckham and Owen made the metatarsal famous, but it's still a broken toe to most people. One night, after a few pints of the guest ale, Old Buffer, I got talking to a couple about their son's reluctance to play school sports. Not being keen on sport themselves, the sympathetic parents bombarded the games teacher with excuses notes on a weekly basis.

After further discussion and a brainstorming session, the three of us came up with the designer injury gift box. In it, you'd find an X-ray, a doctor's note and the medical bandaging required to guarantee your child at least six weeks away from games.

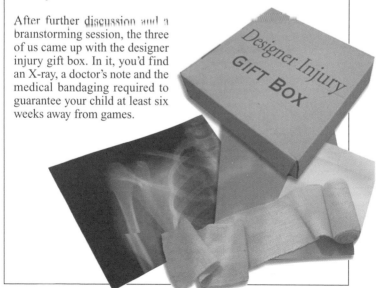

Six Steps to a Perfect Beer Gut

If you're daunted by the training required to get the perfect beer gut, then this simple workout is the one for you. Get yourself spectacularly out of shape by following our easy-to-follow six-step home workout. No gym membership required.

1 The pint crunch

Lie in a relaxed position, preferably within sight of the TV. Gently grip the back of your own neck in one hand and the neck of your chosen drink in the other and then lift both to meet in the middle, without taking your eyes off the TV for a second. Relax and then repeat until the drink is finished.

2 The twisting kebab crunch

Lightly cradle the base of your head with the fingers of both hands and sit up and across towards your preferred snack. Help yourself and then return to the relaxed position. Repeat until most of the snack has been eaten, with the remainder having stained the front of your shirt.

3 The seated pie lift

From your TV viewing vantage point, sit down in your favourite chair and place a pie in your lap. Raise your knees and the pie to your mouth from the seated position and then relax. Keep the repetitions going until the pie has been consumed.

4 Lager lift

In a standing position facing the television, gently squat and drink from alternate pint glasses until both drinks are finished. Remember, the quicker you do this exercise, the sooner it will be over.

Warning You will need two pints for this exercise for balance and to avoid unnecessary muscle strain.

5 Pie lunges

From the upright position, gently roll down through your spine, exhaling through your nose until you reach your pie, then take a bite. Then gently roll slowly back up to the upright position. This exercise is ideally performed while the adverts are on, since performing it correctly may interrupt your viewing pleasure.

6 Pickled-egg plank

The final stage of the workout is perhaps the hardest part of the routine. Ideally you will have someone spotting you for this exercise. Get yourself into a press-up position, using your elbows to hold your weight. You can do this on your toes or on your knees. If you want more of a defined beer gut, I suggest using your knees. Then simply dip your mouth into the picked eggs and repeat until the jar is empty. You may need some-one helping you with the eggs as you get towards the bottom of the jar.

SAFETY INFORMATION

Discuss your general health status with your doctor to ensure that you are healthy enough to engage in this high-intensity workout. If you experience chest pain, nausea or any other discomforts during the workout, stop immediately and seek medical help.

The most common side effects of this workout are headache, upset stomach, facial flushing and flatulence. Less commonly, blurred vision or sensitivity to light from the television may briefly occur.

In rare instances, men and women using this workout have been known to just drop down dead.

If you are above the age of 65, or have serious weight problems, high blood pressure or prostate problems then we don't advise that you take part in this workout.

Common side effects

- Nausea/vomiting
- Psychomotor impairment
- Light-headedness
- Dizziness
- Drowsiness
- Rash
- Dependence/tolerance

WE THEREFORE **DO NOT** RECOMMEND THAT YOU TRY THE 'SIX STEPS TO A PERFECT BEER GUT' WORKOUT UNDER ABSOLUTELY ANY CIRCUMSTANCES.
HAVE A NICE DAY!

Communications

There have been countless revolutions in technology in recent years, no more so than in the field of mobile telephony. This billion-pound industry has spawned a range of accessories and add-ons, including Bluetooth headsets, annoying ringtones, Snake and of course the most important of all — a tiny speaker through which to play crap music for the enjoyment of your fellow commuters. Indecd, many of us appear to be receiving instructional texts from some higher being in order to function properly. Happily tapping away on your mobile keypad, 'C U L8R' takes on a whole new meaning as you step under a bus… So it's this amazing communication technology that has provoked the pub ideas 'discsd in dis chapter, m8'.

SEE FULL-COLOUR IDEA 12

ASBO PHONE LOCK

One Friday night, a remorseful girl told me about a drunken midnight call she had made earlier on in the week:

'Oh God, it's awful. I never should have phoned him and said what I said at that time in the morning.'

'Don't worry,' replied her friend. 'I texted Gary last Sunday morning saying a similar thing.'

Something clearly needed to be done, so our newly formed collective decided to resolve the seemingly universal problem of under-the-influence mobile communication. A few ideas were kicked around: Leave your phone at home and, rather more disturbingly, leave Gary. Fortunately for Gary, these solutions were dismissed as unworkable. The next idea, however, was far more interesting:

'What about a mobile phone with an alcohol-sensitive keypad on it?' suggested one of the girls. 'When you've had more than a certain number of drinks, say three or four, the phone automatically locks itself, preventing you from sending any drunken messages.'

The next day, I forwarded a well-crafted technical diagram (and the beer mat on which it was drawn) to a leading mobile phone manufacturer. Rather surprisingly, I've heard nothing back. Still, we filed an official pub patent (a photocopy of the beer mat) and will sue anyone who even dares replicate the idea without our consortium's say-so.

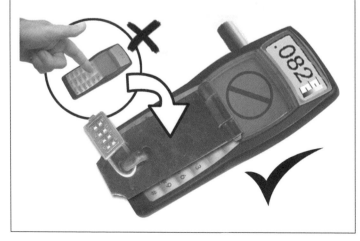

AUTOMATIC APOLOGY TEXT WIZARD

A few days later, I told a group of people in the pub about our consortium's plans to conquer the world with the ASBO phone lock (see previous page). This was offered up as a potential interim solution. Simply enter the names of all the people who you're out with or those whom you're likely to phone in the middle of the night when steaming drunk. Then let the apology wizard do all the work for you, automatically sending 'sorry for being such a tosser' messages to everyone on the list and leaving you to sleep in peace until the hangover disappears the next morning/afternoon.

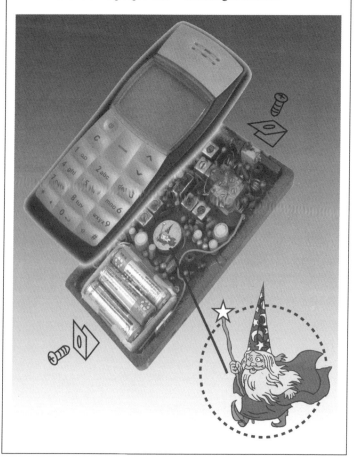

UHHH, I WON'T BE IN TODAY...

The Sick Voice Modulator came about when a girl I was speaking to one evening told me that she'd just received her second written warning for absenteeism. It transpired that she'd phoned in sick on a Monday morning, and her boss had seen through her excuses.

'What would be really useful would be a sick voice modulator. Some sort of voice-altering device to make you sound extremely ill.'

I'm not too sure the girl will keep her job, though, since it might take some time to get this medical technology to the market.

MOBILE PHONE JAMMER

One night, an angry commuter told me about a serial mobile phone pest. Every morning, a suited man would board the quiet coach of the 6:50am train and start barking instructions into his mobile to some poor sod at the other end. The quiet coach of the early-morning train had been the commuter's sanctuary, providing him with an extra hour of sleep. Despite his protestations, however, the offending suit had continued to flout the rules.

'It would be really useful if the rail company fitted the train with a mobile phone jamming device that would shut that bastard up. Or if jamming equipment could be built into your own phone, some kind of Bluetooth signal could be sent to block everyone else's phone.'

Another disgruntled commuter suggested an add-on feature to jam the phone's speaker system as well.

'A group of school kids get on my bus and insist on playing 25p (50 Cent) through a tiny speaker on their phone.'

CONVINCE YOUR PARTNER YOU'RE HAVING AN AFFAIR

One evening, a friend and I were talking to a girl who told us that her boyfriend had become a little complacent. The only time she got to see him was when he was recovering from a night out or watching football with his mates on the TV at home. Although she was still madly in love, she felt that her boyfriend needed a little wake-up call.

'I'd like a service whereby you could convince your partner that you might be having an affair, without actually having one. A call centre, perhaps in India, that would call you up and send you texts in the middle of the

night. They could hang up every time your partner answered, just to add to the mystery.'

Shortly after her announcement, my friend, who had looked somewhat settled in for the evening, downed his pint and raced home. I randomly bumped into his girlfriend the next day.

'I don't know what came over Mark last night, but he came home early from the pub with some flowers. He hadn't even done anything wrong!'

'Ah...' was my response. 'There's no room for complacency in a relationship.'

PARTY CONFERENCE

See full-colour idea 12

You'd be hard pushed to find a bar in London without at least one Aussie member of staff. As a rule of thumb, it's always the one serving you after yet another Aussie sporting victory. On the whole, I've always found our antipodean friends to have an extremely positive outlook on life. One Sunday lunchtime, however, I spotted an unusually glum Aussie regular slumped at the bar. I scoured the back pages of the newspapers for signs of an Australian sporting defeat but found nothing, so I asked him what was wrong. He told me that it was his brother's 25th birthday and that he was missing the party of the century back home.

I bought him a consolation pint and, being Australian, he stood his round, so we toasted his brother with a second. At around the three-pint mark, he struck gold with this amber nectar.

'What would be really cool would be a conference party.'

I thought I knew where he was going with this.

'Like a live video-conferencing link up?' I asked.

'Exactly – that would be awesome. You could set up a conferencing centre with a bar and stuff, play the same music across the two sites and party with your family. Home from home.'

'Brilliant,' I replied. 'You could call it Neighbours.'

'Don't be a nob, Tom.' he replied.

WHAT A TURN-OFF

One night, a woman told me that her husband had left the iron on all day. He'd realized the error on his way to work, but he had an important meeting with his boss and had quickly forgotten again. This hadn't been the first time it had happened.

'What about making household appliances text friendly?' I suggested. 'You could send a text message to your iron, for example, telling it to turn itself off.'

'Single people could reap huge benefits,' the woman added. 'You could text the cooker to start cooking half an hour before leaving the pub and have dinner waiting by the time you get home.'

SLACKBERRY

One evening, I spoke to a very tired-looking woman on her way back home to Wimbledon. She spoke of sleepless nights, having to get up in the middle of the night and how she could barely get through a meal with her husband without interruption. Of course, I assumed that she was talking about the joys of a newborn baby, but in fact she was referring to her SlackBerry hand-held communication device.

These popular business tools harbour all the features you'd find on a PC but are in fact tamagotchi toys for grown-ups. Bleeps, rings and flashing lights demand instant attention, stopping you dead in your tracks, disrupting sleep, romantic meals, sporting events and even pilots making their final approach. How can we convert the nagging hand-held into a positive influence on our lives, I wondered?

My friend sent me the following life-changing pub idea, rather ironically using his trusted SlackBerry.

From: Mac, Jim
Subject: SlackBerry

Ello m8... Thought occurred to me this morning, missed mum's birthday again, made it to all my meetings today though, thanks to the old SlackBerry.

I was thinking, as I always forget birthdays (sorry about yours... was it any good?), weddings, anniversaries and generally all things of importance, what about a communication device that's set up to spend 24 hours a day nagging you about what you should be doing?

————————————?Sent using SlackBerry

From: Waine, Tom
Subject: Re: SlackBerry

Isn't that what a conventional hand-held does?

Birthday, not bad ta. BTW, where are you?

————————————?Sent using SlackBerry

From: Mac, Jim
Subject: Re: Re: SlackBerry

Ah Tom... where my technology differs is in the detail. Not only would the SlackBerry remind you of a pending birthday; it would also check up to see if you had done anything about it yet... offer gift suggestions, make sure you've got stamps so that you can get the card away on time, etc...

I'm in the Plough.

————————————?Sent using SlackBerry

From: Waine, Tom
Subject: Re: Re: Re: SlackBerry

Brilliant Jim, now are you coming down to the Royal Oak? I'm only 150 yards away?

Tom

————————————?Sent using SlackBerry

E-MAIL OFFENCE DECRYPTION SOFTWARE

On the one rare occasion I was sat at home on a Friday night, one of my friends sent me a distraught e-mail from the pub using her SlackBerry.

From: Emma H
Subject: I think I'm going to get sacked – Message (Plain Text)
Date: Tue 16/01/2007 15:55:31
To: Tom Waine

Hi Tom
Oh shit, I sent an e-mail to my boss and didn't check it properly. His name is Angus and I missed out the g :-Z

It read:

———Original message———
From: Emma H
Subject: Finished
Sent: Tue 16/01/2007 15:45:12
To: Angus McDoe

Anus
I worked through my lunch break to get everything done today, so could I leave a bit earlier?
Emma

———————————?Sent using SlackBerry

My response was short and to the point.

From: Tom Waine
Subject: Re: I think I'm going to get sacked – Message (Plain Text)
Date: Tue 16/01/ 2007 18:50:55
To: Emma H
Let's hope your boss isn't e-maily retentive. See you down the pub in 15 mins.
Tom

——————————?Sent using SlackBerry

Once in the safety of the pub, we discussed the pitfalls of e-mailing, and the results were conclusive. One slip on the keyboard, a misplaced comma, the wrong smiley icon or a simple character omission, could land the e-mail author in a whole lot of trouble.

The solution: E-mail Offence Decryption Software

Software to decode smiley faces, bad punctuation and author intent. It could run through an e-mail in a similar way to a simple spellcheck but would decipher both the author's mood and their motivation, thus negating misunderstandings.

In this case, the decryption software wasn't required. It transpired that Emma's boss had a sense of humour and, apparently, it wasn't the first time that he had been called an asshole.

PERSONAL GROOMING

Personal grooming is big business. Manicures, pedicures and spa treatments are no longer exclusive to just the fairer sex. Since a famous shaggy-haired football player told us that he was worth it, men and women, it would seem, are now equally obsessed with the world of hand creams, hair dyes and waxing. The overgrown look, I'm reliably informed, died with the merkin (pubic toupee). Over the last few years, I've grouped together some of my favourite pub personal-grooming ideas. All of them sit in this chapter as naturally and as painlessly as the recipient of a back, crack and sack wax.

SEE FULL-COLOUR IDEA 13

SUIT VENDING MACHINE

See full-colour idea 13

It was a cold Saturday night in December when I heard this priceless gem from a scruffy-looking American Express employee. Having missed the last train home after his Christmas party, the drunken reveller spent the night curled up under his desk. With no change of clothes at work, he spent the next day at work wearing the same shabby suit. And, to make matters worse, he was due for dinner with his still-furious girlfriend and her parents that night. With a pint of his favourite Old Mottled Cock in hand, he was bracing himself for the worst when this spark of inspiration struck:

'What would've been really handy is a vending machine that sells you a suit, shirt and new tie. They could be situated at every station and come in a variety of sizes. For £20 you could have a new outfit.'

'Lots of people miss their last train home and sleep under their desk, right?'

I nodded in agreement, of course, but I wasn't too sure his girlfriend would be so easily convinced.

CLUB SHOES

See full-colour idea 13

An excited group of revellers sat down at the table beside me one Friday night, warming up with a few pints before heading off to club land to see a famous DJ. An hour later, one of the group trudged back through the door, looking thoroughly hacked off. I asked him what had happened.

'It's pathetic. The bouncer turned me away because I'm wearing white trainers,' he said glumly. 'Everyone else got in except me.'

Resigned to the fact that he wasn't going to find any suitable shoes that evening, we came up with the perfect solution for future club footwear catastrophes. Next to the suit-vending machine should be a similar machine bearing the name Club Shoes. For £5, you could get a pair of club-friendly pumps complete with a rucksack in which to conceal the offending trainers.

We sat and toasted his idea over a few more pints. Then, on the stroke of midnight, in piled the rest of his friends, looking even more pissed off than he had when he returned. Apparently, the famous DJ had not made his flight. Perhaps airport security had taken exception to his shoes?

TELESCOPIC HEEL STILETTOS

A girl sat down next to me one evening and kicked off her shoes, bitterly complaining about the hassle of wearing heels to work. I asked her what she'd rather wear. The problem wasn't wearing the heels at work, per se, it was the travelling to and from work while wearing them that caused the pain. When I suggested that she could wear trainers for the commute and change when she got to work, she told me that she only had a small bag and in any case needed footwear that was both practical and sexy in the event of an impromptu night out.

'What would be ideal,' she continued, 'would be telescopic heels. That way you could walk to work in flat shoes, extend them, spend the day in heels and flatten them out again for the walk home!'

STEALTH EARRINGS

Over a few midweek pints, I listened to a married couple talking about their teenage son. He'd been sent home from school for wearing an earring. The teenager had paid with his own money to have the piercing done, and he was worried that the hole would close up if he had to remove his earring for school. The couple's solution to the dilemma was the Stealth Earring.

Choose from a range of studs that resemble zits, moles or birthmarks. Problem solved! There were, of course, other applications for this slice of pub genius.

◆ **Meeting your in-laws (without the earring)**

◆ **Meeting your own parents (have you told them about the nose ring?)**

◆ **Meeting your prospective employer (a nipple chain might thwart your chances of becoming a life guard)**

DIY HOME TATTOO KITS

The subject of tattoos came up during a pub session with work colleagues one evening. Everyone had an opinion on the matter, but the shocking revelation came from one of the quieter office girls. She'd always been intrigued by tattoos and desperately wanted to get one, but she found her local tattoo parlour too intimidating. Ever practical in such situations, Steve, a visiting Canadian colleague, suggested the DIY home tattoo kit. Each kit should contain the following:

◆ **A prosthetic leg for practice before taking the plunge on one of your own limbs.**

◆ **Dyslexic dictionary to ensure any spelling is wrong.**

◆ **Stencils of the classic designs (skull, rose, Mum, Britney, etc...).**

Remember, a tattoo is for life, not just for Christmas!

TRICKY HAIR
Spa & Gym

'Because your body deserves the <u>best</u>'

SPECIAL DEALS THIS MONTH
Styling
Croydon face lift £2.50

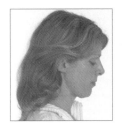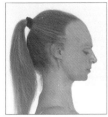

Beauty & health
Retox treatments – *Brewery and distillery tours from* **£29.99**

Scottish Tanning System – *Flawless pasty white complexion from only* **£9.99**

Back, crack and sack wax – Priceless!

Gym & SPA
Personal training and development courses include:*
- *Running for the bus with a cigarette in your mouth*
- *Stealth pissing in the pool or jacuzzi*
- *Fart avoidance on the massage table*

*All free if you join this month

Tricky Plastic

AESTHETIC IMPERFECTION SURGERY

'Life's hard enough without having to suffer beautiful friends...'

Treat someone special to some surgery to even things out a little.

Pile on the pounds with some reverse liposuction

Treat your best mate to our Manilow nose extension

25% off laser-induced hair loss and teeth yellowing

CALL 01632 555 5555 FOR MORE DETAILS

Sport & Leisure

The pursuit of sport and leisure has long been a national obsession — a way to unwind and escape the rigmarole of the working week. Some people escape the big city and find solace climbing a mountain, while others work up a sweat in the local gym. For those of us who take refuge in the lounge bar of the local boozer, the discussion of sport and leisure is never far from the agenda. Every weekend we become authorities, talking of places we intend to visit and sports we'll start in the New Year. As soon as the big match graces the pub widescreen TV, we're all armchair experts, discussing our unfulfilled potential as we knock back the next pint and smoke like a chimney. With this in mind, I've collected some of the nation's favourite ideas on the ever-popular topic of sport and leisure.

SEE FULL-COLOUR IDEAS 14 AND 15

FOUR-LETTER DAYS

I got speaking to someone in the pub one night who turned out to be a recent recipient of an adventure-activity gift. The girl's friends had chipped in to provide her with a Sunday afternoon's hot-air ballooning. Unfortunately, not only did the reluctant recipient suffer from vertigo, she was also an avid football fan and would miss her team's big match that day. For that reason, the person shall remain anonymous, so as not to appear ungrateful to her generous friends. I asked her what she would have preferred had she been able to choose her own day out. Her reply was fantastic:

'I've had this idea for a while. It's kind of like the sporting equivalent of reality TV, where you get dropped right in the thick of some very exciting sporting action.'

She then proceeded to give me a number of examples:

◆ **The 5th test of the Ashes. You're suddenly the middle order batsman on a pitch that's turning, with Shane Warne bowling the next over (let's face it, a lot of us could do better).**

◆ **You're brought on as goalie for a team five-nil up at half time during the FA Cup. (Imagine the hairdryer experience you'd receive in the dressing room at the end of 90 minutes if you went on to lose the game.)**

◆ **Last-minute addition to a crew of the Oxford and Cambridge Boat Race.**

◆ **Rugby World Cup final. England leads Australia by 2 points in the dying seconds of the game. Now you're the full back.**

I got the picture. I suggested to her that if ballooning wasn't exhilarating enough, perhaps she could take her own bungee cord next time.

BED-LETTER DAYS

We all have those over-active, annoying friends who like to tire us out by talking about what they did last weekend – tales of white-water rafting, skydiving jaunts, that kind of thing. Let's put them back in their place with a Bed-Letter Day. All you need is one old bed, a TV remote, a voucher for the local pizza delivery service and instructions for them to sit and do bugger all for the entire weekend.

SATURDAY AFTERNOON SEANCE

Every Saturday afternoon, millllons of football fans sit glued to the videprinter on TV as the full-time scores roll in from around the country. One particular Saturday I was in the pub, staring at the tiny flashing asterisk along with everyone else, when the wife of the friend I was with burst into the room. Various expletives were exchanged, along with comparisons to animals much further down the food chain than ourselves. My friend then let out a groan – his team had gone one-nil down – which did little to placate his wife. He then made his excuses and followed his wife out, still keeping one eye firmly fixed on the flashing asterisk.

With all the scores in, the pub suddenly came back to life, and I found myself surrounded by a mixture of smiling and shell-shocked fans. I asked whether anyone else had noticed the woman come in and tear a strip off her husband. Only one guy nodded, and we got talking. It turns out that he'd shared a similar experience several weeks before:

'My wife came into the lounge a few weeks ago and started throwing dirty socks at me until she had grabbed my full attention. Why hadn't I picked her up from the shops as she'd asked me to? "I don't know, Smudge," she said. "If I really wanted to get you to do anything on a Saturday, I'd have to text the BBC and get a message to you via the

videprinter: <Smudge, you're late! Where are you? It's my birthday tomorrow, so buy me something.>"'.

Subliminal messaging via the medium of videprinter; just think what could be achieved. . .

VICARIOUS CLUBBING

The idea for vicarious clubbing came from a group of pub revellers celebrating their friend's 35th birthday. The celebration was fairly tame, with the group enjoying some food and a few pints while reminiscing over misspent youth. It turned out that the guest of honour's 30th birthday party had been an altogether different affair – a debauched pub crawl starting at midday and ending up in a night-club at 6am the following morning. It transpired that many of the group had subsequently married and settled down and no longer had the stamina to stay up for club nights.

'I still quite fancy the idea of going clubbing,' claimed one girl, 'But I'm just too tired and would rather go home and put my feet up.'

Discussions on the merit of this statement ensued – the general consensus was homeward bound, but it provoked the following excellent pub idea:

Vicarious Clubbing

An interactive clubbing website for the over 30s. Subscription payment allows punters to party the night away from the comfort of their own home. Simply log into the website, select a clubber for the night (from a list of eager students) and tell them what to do.

Drink one of these shooters >

Chat him/her up >

Request your favourite dance anthem >

Extra chilli sauce on the kebab, please >

Kiss him/her goodnight >

Duck to avoid the slap >

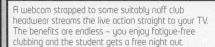

A webcam strapped to some suitably naff club headwear streams the live action straight to your TV. The benefits are endless – you enjoy fatigue-free clubbing and the student gets a free night out.

STAY-AT-HOME CAMPING SERVICE

Can't afford to camp or are you just too lazy to pitch a tent? Ring the Stay-at-Home Camping Service hotline and our response unit will be with you in minutes. Our team will make the following adjustments to recreate a genuine camping experience:

Unplug the fridge so that all your food goes out of date overnight

❖

Disable all but one ring on your cooker

❖

Release all manner of creepy crawlies into your bedroom

❖

Get someone to fall over your bed every 20 minutes during the night

❖

Keep you awake by playing crap folk songs until 4am

❖

Replace your dining room furniture with uncomfortable garden chairs
and a plastic table that collapses every time you lean on it

❖

Carefully dampen all towels and clothing

❖

Block your toilet

❖

Knock over every cup of tea you make with a well-aimed Frisbee throw

❖

Litter the house with cowpats

See full-colour idea 14

OCD CLEANING SERVICE

Suffer from obsessive-compulsive disorder?
Going on holiday? Need a cleaner?
We guarantee to outdo your cleaning neuroses.

- Your house will be spotless
- Everything will smell of bleach
- Every item replaced in exactly the same way as we found it
- Lost items stay lost – What else would you have to worry about?
- Cleaning products arranged in neat height order ready for immediate use when you return.

MURDER ON THE ORIENT EXPRESS (CHEAP AWAY-DAY)

I was sitting in a bar in Waterloo, contemplating my pending cattle-class journey up to the Midlands, when the *Orient Express* drew up in the sidings. Marvelling at the sheer luxury of the locomotive, I couldn't help wonder if I'd ever be able to afford such a high-class train adventure. 'Murder on the Midlands Express,' although a distinct possibility, doesn't quite have the same ring to it as Agatha Christie's 1974 classic. I discussed the possibility of a modern-day version of the film with a weary-looking commuter sitting at the next table. He didn't think the film had legs, but he did offer this suggestion:

'Perhaps the Orient Express *could offer some sort of cheap away-day breaks for the working classes – a whistle-stop tour of some of our wonderful towns and cities, a scenic tour of Slough, Swindon and Southampton, for example. All you'd need is two coaches. Standing room only, of course, with a mobile trolley serving stale cheese sandwiches and cheap continental lager for double the price of the ticket.'*

I had a feeling that my new friend was perhaps becoming disillusioned with his daily commute and, as yet, haven't contacted the *Orient Express* with his idea.

WINTER SOLSTICE FESTIVAL AT GLASTONBURY

Following his return from yet another washed-out summer festival, my brother and I were catching up over a couple of pints. He was, of course, full of cold but between sneezes he mustered this priceless piece of irony:

'They should do a winter solstice music festival. You could almost guarantee better weather – or at least consistent rain, sleet or snow.'

'Go on,' I prompted.

'Well, first off, it'd be much easier to get tickets. I'd hold the festival in a cowshed so all you'd need to bring is a sleeping bag. Food stalls could sell mulled wine, hot cider and even Christmas dinner, and there'd be plenty of fires and braziers to keep you warm. Michael Eavis (Glastonbury landowner and festival organiser) could even dress up as Santa.'

'So,' I said after a moment's quiet reflection, 'I take it you'll be giving next year's summer festivals a miss then?'

'Not a chance.'

TOO POSH TO PITCH

Wimbledon – the pinnacle of the ATP tennis tour. For some fans, it's tennis at its finest; for others, it's simply a place to be seen. For the third year in a row, two tennis-mad friends of mine camped at the ticket office overnight but failed to secure tickets. Armed with a pint of Roger & Out to dull their disappointment, they offered the following thoughts on improving the chances of getting tickets for the bloody event.

Wealth day at Wimbledon

For most of the two-week run, Wimbledon tickets would go on sale to the general public, paid for at the gate on a first-come, first-served basis. However, one day would be reserved for extremely wealthy people, who could pitch their tents and queue through the night for the chance to pay £25,000 for a ticket. True to form, their tickets could then be sold on to the general public, following their one glass of champagne in the Member's Bar.

F1 HAULAGE

See full-colour idea 15

This idea came about a few years ago while drinking a pint of Cornish Knocker in a pub in Tavistock, watching the Grand Prix with a few of the locals. The race was dominated by one of the drivers, and the result was looking a bit academic. At this point, one of the locals (a long-distance lorry driver) offered up the following gem of an idea:

'I'd like to see 'em drive a lorry for a living,' he exclaimed. 'Let's see how they'd cope with avoiding all the bloody speed cameras or trying to use a taco-graph – that'd sort out the real drivers!'

As is often the way down in Cornwall, the whole pub got involved in the discussion. Instead of high-performance vehicles, the F1 drivers would be given lorries fitted with taco-graphs for the season. They would race the same F1 circuits, but on tracks littered with speed cameras and transport cafés. Drivers would have to keep within the 56mph speed limit for the entire season. During the race, drivers would be required to make at least two 'piss stops', consume two all-day breakfasts, smoke 40 rollups (two of which should be rolled while driving) and make 16 calls on a mobile. As in the current F1 series, the winner would be the first driver over the line. After each race, the Department for Transport would check the taco-graphs and speed cameras, awarding time penalties and points on licences for breaking speed limits. At the end of the season, the overall winner would be the driver with the least points on their licence, the most race wins and the heaviest overall bodyweight.

THE SCORE – PUB LEAGUE ROUND-UP

The next bit of sporting fuzzy logic came from a disillusioned football fan sitting in the pub one Sunday afternoon. After reading of his Premiership team's dismal run of fortune, Dave decided he would be better off reading about his local pub team's results. Further discussion resulted in the idea of a Pub League round-up in the sports section of the Sunday papers.

REF SEES RED AS SOUTHAMPTON ARMS PULLS IN AT STATION

SOUTHAMPTON ARMS 1 *(OG) Mick 46'*
STATION HOTEL 0

THE SOUTHAMPTON ARMS started off this Boxing Day grudge match in a positive manner but lost their brightest player to the christening of his nephew at half time. His hungover replacement entered the fray with immediate impact, hitting a stunning 15-yard deflection off the over-indulgent gut of the Station Hotel central defender.

Station Hotel's manager was quick to respond, with a double substitution of his two lacklustre strikers, whose fitness was always in doubt following a 2am finish at the local nightclub. The Station team then commanded the midfield for the next three and a half minutes, until the game descended into chaos. Southampton Arms' striker mistimed his full nelson on the flat-footed Station Hotel defender, leaving the referee, a retired dentist, with no option but to produce the red card.

A flurry of bookings then followed as the ref struggled to regain control of the game. Three minutes from time, the dismissed Southampton Arms forward decided to put himself back into the action, this time behind the wheel of his Ford Cortina. Narrowly missing an opportunity to connect with the referee in the six-yard area, instead he connected with one of his own team, adding considerably to the injury worries of the Southampton Arms landlord/manager. The game finished 1-0 to the Southampton Arms.

Attendance: 6, plus 2 dogs

The CREATORS OF championship manager are proud to announce the start of the new Sunday League Manager season

CHOOSE FROM THOUSANDS OF SUNDAY LEAGUE & PUB TEAMS

REALISTIC PLAYER STATISTICS INCLUDE CRIMINAL CONVICTIONS

TAKE YOUR PUB TEAM TO THE DIZZY HEIGHTS OF THE RYMANS LEAGUE!

Available in shops 2nd December

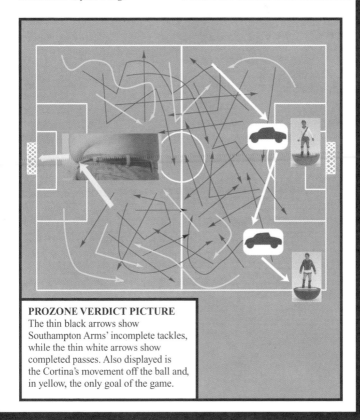

PROZONE VERDICT PICTURE
The thin black arrows show Southampton Arms' incomplete tackles, while the thin white arrows show completed passes. Also displayed is the Cortina's movement off the ball and, in yellow, the only goal of the game.

MISCELLANEOUS MADNESS

The gravity and hangover of some of the ideas in this chapter led me to question my own understanding of the word 'idea'. Consultation with the Oxford English Dictionary returned the following detailed definitions:

'The mental process of knowing, including aspects such as awareness, perception, reasoning, and judgement.'

During the course of my research, awareness, judgement and reasoning had not always been in abundance as the bell rang for last orders although that, of course, could just be my perception.

'Something, such as a thought or conception, that potentially or actually exists in the mind as a product of mental activity.'

Again, the correlation between mental activity and the amount of pints consumed left me somewhat cold with this particular definition. I think the most exacting description was the last one I stumbled upon:

'A mental image of something remembered.'

I'll leave you to ponder over its brevity as you piece together the pages of the penultimate chapter.

SEE FULL-COLOUR IDEA 16

TRICKY AIR

As I sat talking to my friend Rich in the pub one Friday night, it soon became apparent that he wasn't too happy about his travel arrangements to Ireland the next day. In her infinite wisdom, Rich's girlfriend booked them on a major airline from the nearest and most convenient airport. It turned out that Rich was hoping for a bit more adventure. No-frills flying with the following features:

◆ **Departure airport in the middle of nowhere with no direct transport links**

◆ **Delays of at least 3 hours, rendering your 4am start a complete waste of time**

◆ **£2 flight each way plus £200 tax (each way)**

◆ **Patronizing airline staff**

◆ **Crap food available if you can pay in a currency you don't have**

◆ **Destination airport at least 200 miles from your hotel**

◆ **All major credit cards not accepted**

◆ **Damage to and/or loss of personal belongings guaranteed**

'That's the sort of airline I want to fly with' insisted Rich.

I tried to console him, but the fact that his journey was going to be so uncomplicated was clearly troubling him. However, the sort of airline he was looking for wasn't a million miles away – in fact, about three train journeys and a taxi ride from the pub. Rich still had time to make a few changes to his travel itinerary.

TRICKY VET

See full-colour idea 16

On the following Saturday night, I was discussing the Tricky Air idea with a friend called Paul. After a few minutes, careful consideration, Paul came up with his own addition to the Tricky brand.

'How about a budget veterinary practice for your pets? Book your dog in for an operation without weighing it and then weigh it on the way out. If your pet is over the "baggage allowance," you'll have to pay the excess.'

Paul was 'in the zone' on his second pint of Boondoggle. He then ordered a third, referring to it by its lesser-known name, Googledog somewhat fitting in the context of his idea.

BOOK OF BULLSHIT ACRONYMS (BBSA)

In a pub in London Bridge at the end of the nineties, I witnessed an idea borne out of pure anger and frustration, voiced after the rapid consumption of a cold glass of Duvel. Earlier in the day, our incensed (and anonymous) employee attended a meeting choreographed by a group of management consultants. What he witnessed was a meeting conducted entirely in a strange alien language – a language so complex that not even the Enigma machine could crack it. A meeting using acronyms of dazzling complexity and tightly woven together with some clever Powerpoint wizardry. Stunned into silence, he left the meeting and headed straight for the pub. Within the arena of All Bar One, and armed with four pints of London Pride, the employee let fly with his WOMD (Weapon of Mass Destruction):

'What about a BBSA: a Book of BullShit Acronyms! Add your own confusing acronyms to the melting pot and rival the best the management consultants have to offer. Rise up against the machines and play them at their own game.'

I approached a number of leading management consultancies, WARTC (who all refused to comment).

E-MAIL MAT

A couple sat in the pub one Sunday, reflecting on the dance-mat injuries that occurred at their friend's party the night before. It had been a strenuous evening of dance, and both were feeling the physical effects. The guy, an office manager who was slightly overweight (according to his wife), had been working all day, dutifully catching up on his e-mails. While contemplating her husband's e-mail mountain and bulky frame, the woman imparted the following pub idea:

'You enjoyed the dance-mat game last night, didn't you, dear?' she asked.

'Of course,' assured her husband.

'Then what you need is a keyboard mat,' she continued.

'A what?' he replied.

'A keyboard mat,' she repeated. 'Simply plug the mat into your computer and then tap away on it with your feet. Then you could exercise while clearing your e-mails.'

LAUNDERETTE SINGLES BAR

If you've ever had to endure an evening in the launderette, you'll understand why psychologists have long been trying to prove the link between launderette use and manic depression. Packed to capacity on a Monday or Wednesday night, the long, bleak wait between cycles is comparable to watching an A-Level theatre-group production of *Waiting For Godot*. This life-squandering pastime, when paired with depressing statistics regarding the disappearance of socks (see Global Positioning Socks, Chapter 1), led our then-single pub genius, Cathy, to chance upon the following pub idea.

'What about a launderette with a bar in it?' she exclaimed. 'Even better, a launderette singles' night. You could even organize a speed-dating session between your whites and your coloured washes.'

Further to this stroke of genius, Cathy came up with the idea of a VIP area for people waiting for their service wash. We can only wait to see whether Cathy's idea takes off.

BRITAIN – THE PRIVATE COMPANY

This discussion started off as a serious debate one evening down the local. Someone suggested that we could do away with corrupt politicians and get Richard Branson to run the country. All he needed was the help of a publicly appointed team of directors in charge of the different departments. As the drinks flowed, the list of who we would choose was quite radically revised…

Position	Original appointment	Last orders appointment
MD	Richard Branson	Sven-Göran Eriksson
Deputy MD	Alan Sugar	Whoever's under Sven (insert her name here)
FD	Roman Abramovich	Nick Leeson
Culture, Spin and Propaganda	Max Clifford	Tony Blair
War (Defence)	Garry Kasparov	John Terry
Education	Carol Vorderman	Pink Floyd
Health	Jamie Oliver	Pete Doherty
Foreign Office	Bob Geldof	Bernard Manning
Industry	James Dyson	China
Transport	Jeremy Clarkson	John 'Two Jags' Prescott
Work and Pensions	Jeremy Paxman	Peter Stringfellow
Sport	Gary Lineker	Johnny Vegas
Home Affairs	Ken Livingstone	Hugh Hefner, Abu Hamza al-Masri or Handy Andy

CERTIFIED ADS

£ ITEMS FOR SALE £

Girlfriend/Boyfriend Hampers

Your very own basket case. Persuade your friends/mother that you have a girlfriend/boyfriend with one of our convincing hampers.

For a Girlfriend
- Photo
- Hair band
- Toothbrush
- Love letter
- Underwear
- Hairdryer
- Pissed-off message on a Post-it

For a Boyfriend
- Underwear with holes in arse
- Odd socks
- Pubic hair for the bathroom
- PS2 with games to scatter around the living room
- Smelly trainers

Packs can be tailor-made to meet your specific requirement.

Only £4.99
Streatham 01632 555 3555

Human Parcel Service

Send yourself or an annoying colleague anywhere in the world

ISLINGTON 01632 545 5555

Kangerees

Supermarket transportation device for mothers with newborns. Not dissimilar from dungarees but modelled on a kangaroo, Kangerees come with springy shoes to get you to the checkouts quicker. Boxing gloves provided to fend off queue jumpers.

Call Karen, Finsbury Park
01632 5555 545

Fancy Dresser

Perfect for stag and hen parties Choose your theme and we'll organize costumes, transport, etc…

Special deals
- Scooby Doo mystery-tour bus hire complete with all costumes and driver, £150
- A-Team van and costume hire, complete with BA Baracus driver, £150

Call 01632 5555 445 for more information

CERTIFIED ADS

CERTIFIED ADS

✈ Health & Travel ✈

Delhi Belly Tours

Diet holidays to India

Free phone **01632 555 5555**
for a brochure.

Eyesore Tours

WHY PAY OVER
THE ODDS?
Combine budget laser eye
surgery with a sightseeing
tour of Eastern Europe. You
might be disappointed, so do
your sightseeing first!

**Blackburn
01632 545 5555**

ARTICLES WANTED

Annoying TV personality scanning device wanted

I need a scanner that will alert me
to an annoying celebrity's presence
on TV in case I encounter them
while channel-surfing.

Please help!

Kensington 01632 555 4455

Shark Wetsuit

*Anyone got a wetsuit
that makes me look like
a shark in case I get
attacked while surfing?*

**Call
Melbourne 01632 555 5555**

REMOTE CONTROL WANTED

I'm looking for a remote to switch off my neighbour's
strimmer and lawnmower on Sunday mornings. Must also work
on road-working equipment and noisy barbeque guests.

Camden 01632 545 4545

PUB THEORIES

It seems that pubs, bars and clubs are not only fertile grounds for incredible ideas; they're also the incubators for paranoid thoughts and conspiracy theories. Often, there's someone lurking in the local pub with an accent you can't quite put your finger on. They stand in silence, supping on a pint and waiting to divulge their latest theory to anyone who'll listen. I've been privileged to bear witness to some of the best conspiracy theories there are on offer, and I've recorded a few of them for consideration in this chapter.

SEE FULL-COLOUR IDEA 1

TALES FROM THE CIRCLE LINE

This theory didn't exactly originate in a pub, *per se*, but you can bet your bottom dollar a lot of alcohol was consumed prior to telling us about it. A friend and I were on our way back from Farringdon one night. We were sitting minding our own business on the Circle Line, when out of the corner of my eye I spotted someone staring at me from across the carriage. I had caught the eye of a tube nutter. After a couple of stops, he lurched across from the corner and began his patter. It took just a few seconds to work out the guy was utterly pissed. His English was incoherent, and his shabby old suit would have benefited from a suit-vending machine (see Chapter 7). He pointed to the chair next to mine and then sat down.

'Are you going home?'

'Err, yeah,' was my nervous reply.

'Are you going home on the Cirrrcle Liiine?' he repeated at least three times, before we realized he was talking about the Underground.

'Yes, we are on the Circle Line.'

'Well, BEWARE...' he bellowed.

'Why?' my mate countered.

'Because it gets you pissed!' he shouted.

The Leffe from our pub visit that evening was beginning to wear off, so we shot him a puzzled stare.

The man explained that the Circle Line somehow conspired to get any of its passengers completely plastered.

'Perhaps the can of extra-strength cider might be a contributory factor?' I quizzed, pointing to the can in his hand.

My friend cut into the conversation and, to my amazement, started to agree with our shit-faced theorist.

'Tell me about it!' said my mate. *'I've fallen asleep after a few beers a couple of times myself, I'm sure that the Circle Line was to blame.'*

'Aye... I've been stuck on it for years. It's a right bastard!'

The man downed the rest of his can, stumbled to his feet and alighted at Tower Hill, leaving us to reflect on this parting shot:

'DON'T GO NEAR THE CIRCLE LINE. IT'S BAAAD NEWS.'

ODD SOCK CONSPIRACY

A friend offered up the following theory following a discussion on the problem of odd socks one night in my local.

'Bastard socks are the result of a chemical traceable in all washing powders.'

Several years ago, a well-known washing-powder manufacturer was forced to withdraw their washing powder due to an H_2O_2 activator called manganese.

'In tests, manganese was found to cause fabric damage,' informed Stan, our biology teacher-cum-conspiracy theorist for the evening.

He even took the time to draw the complex on a beer mat:

Stan's knowledge stunned and scared us into silence as he continued:

'Apparently, a few of these companies are major shareholders with some well-known sock companies. They've developed an agent that can biologically transform socks into congealed lottery tickets or receipts.'

Our collective tried not to laugh at Stan's animated theory. He was, after all, deadly serious.

'You may laugh,' he protested. *'But who regulates these companies? We've got Offgem for gas and Offcom for telecommunications, but there's not Oddsock to regulate the detergent companies, is there?'*

At this point, the whole table disintegrated into laughter and Stan retreated to the bar. Only then did I notice that Stan was wearing one sock.

SOMETHING FOR THE WEEKEND?

Talking to complete strangers somehow doesn't seem quite so unusual in the comfort of a pub. While conversations about the weather are commonplace, every now and then you'll strike up a priceless conversation with a complete stranger.

One night in a pub in Brighton, a man with an insane mop of

hair came over to my table and introduced himself as Fred. Fred stood silent, staring at me for a while, as I nervously flicked through the sports supplement of the Sunday paper.

'Everything OK, mate?' I asked him, after three minutes of silence.

'Which barber do you go to?' he replied, sitting down at my table.

'Why do you ask?' I said.

He drew his chair closer and lowered his voice. *'I want to get my hair cut but I'm afraid of what they might do.'*

'I see,' was my response. And I really could see.

Anyone familiar with St James' Street in Brighton will be aware that this kind of conversation is quite normal, so I indulged him.

'I have a theory,' he whispered.

'What's that?' I responded.

'How many barbers were there in the shop?'

'Three. Why?' I answered.

'Did he have a good haircut?'

'It was alright.'

Fred took a large swig from his pint glass. With sweaty palms, he then relived his last harrowing hairdressing experience. I couldn't

determine how long ago this was, and I didn't want to push him. It transpired that he was biding his time before his next haircut.

'I've been to a few hairdressers in the past few weeks to study form. I think I've come up with a winning formula.'

'Go on,' I said, patiently.

'You should always pick the barber with the worst haircut.'

'Why's that?' I replied.

'Cos one of the other barbers has cut it for him.'

With that he bolted for the door. I don't know if he ever went for that haircut, but his brilliant theory has saved my scalp on a number of occasions.

CHRISTMAS PRESENT RECYCLING

One evening down the pub early in the New Year, a friend of mine pulled me aside to tell me about something that had been bothering him. He'd got it into his head that, more often than not, his friends and family hadn't actually liked the Christmas presents he'd given them over the years.

'I've been looking into the statistics, and at least 15 per cent of all Christmas presents are returned every year.'

'You've got too much time on your hands,' I replied.

A computer programmer by trade, he told me he was intending to write some ingenious software to see if any of the presents he had given to people appeared on any of the numerous Internet auction websites. He would enter in the name of the recipient, a full description of the gift and its value. His program would then monitor all the auction sites and produce a detailed report of any items matching the information provided. The program would then monitor any sales of these items and work out if any unwanted gifts generated a profit. He would then e-mail his friends or family an invoice, claiming the profit back as his own, along with a frosty message informing them that they had been struck off his Christmas present list.

Astounded, I told him he was being both paranoid and miserable and that any time he wanted to come round and see the wall-mounted singing cod he had bought me last Christmas he would be more than welcome.

ASHES CHIP AND PIN

I'd booked a day off work to watch the Ashes series live from Australia. What better place to watch it than on the widescreen down at my local, I thought. So I headed down to the pub at 9.30 am. The fact that it was so early makes this conspiracy, and the fragile state of the theorist's mind, all the more concerning.

It was a whitewash, and a desperate fan came over to mourn the loss of yet another England wicket. He shared his conspiracy theory, leaving me in

no uncertain terms as to what had gone wrong. All was not right in the England cricket camp.

'No shit,' I replied.

'I'm sure England coach Troy Cooley has got something to do with this,' he continued.

The English coaching staff had poached Troy Cooley back from the Australian team after the last Ashes defeat.

'What do you mean? That Troy has relayed England's tactics to the Australians ahead of the Ashes series?' I asked, incredulously.

He told me he thought it ran much deeper than that. The coach, with the help of a physio (also Australian, apparently), had put the England players under anaesthetic, implanting electronic chips into their brains to suppress their cricketing skills.

I stared at the theorist open-mouthed as Shane Warne collected yet another scalp on the widescreen TV above us. For a split second, I entertained his theory. Although it was complete madness, it did momentarily help to soothe some of the pain.

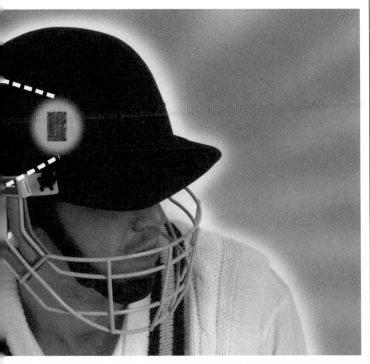

DRIVE BYs

Sometimes, a snapshot of a conversation across a crowded bar will stop you dead in your tracks and make you think. Here are just a few of the snippets of chat I've heard over the years…

Someone called Tim, 11.45 Saturday night: 'You see, I've often thought that vodka is a government experiment in tele-portation. If I've drunk enough of the stuff, and I've got a long walk home, it takes roughly 14 steps before I suddenly find myself in bed feeling sick and dizzy.'

Someone called David, who looked strangely familiar, 9.15 at the bar: 'I believe that the colour purple helps me talk to the Lord directly.'

Mate 1: 'I was told that Basil Brush was a member of the KGB during the Cold War. His code name was Arctic Fox.'
Mate 2: 'Boom boom!'

Someone called Tom, queuing for cider at Great British Beer Festival: 'Countless boy-band cover versions have massacred many good, classic songs. There should be a building listings system for music. Depending on their relative merits, let's designate songs as Grade 1 listed, Grade 2 listed, or not listed at all. In order to release a cover version, you would have to consult a special committee and convince them that you'll be able to do it in a manner sympathetic to the original, thus saving consumers' ears from the sort of crap we're subjected to down the pub on a nightly basis.'

Unknown foreign student talking about Geoffrey Boycott's commentary of an international game: 'I'm telling you, that accent's Australian.'

Unknown artist in leather trousers talking into his mobile in a bar: 'A Priory for stars that can't hold their drink, they book into a retreat for two weeks, unable to leave until they are adept at drinking like fish and hitting paparazzi.'

Pissed-off girl apologising to someone for being late: 'Buses should have a countdown clock. I'm fed up of running the last 20 yards to catch a bus, with the driver smirking as he pulls away. If there was a countdown clock on the front of every bus, you could work out whether to run or not.'

CONSPIRASUDOKU

See full-colour idea opposite

This carefully constructed Conspirasudoku provides you with a different conspiracy theory in every direction! Revel in the magic of Suduko as you come up with yet another theory to wow your friends!

CONSPIRASUDOKU

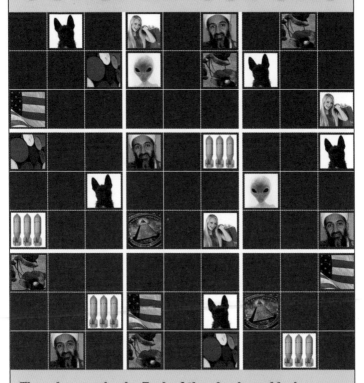

The rules are simple. Each of the nine large black squares must contain all the conspiracy icons, numbered 1 to 9. Each icon can only appear once in a row, column or square. Within the larger square, you must ensure that each nine-square column or row contains the icons 1 to 9 without repeating or omitting an icon.

1	2	3	4	5	6	7	8	9
Area 51	Bin Laden	George W. Bush	Spit the Dog	WMD	Blonde bimbo	Oil	Afghan poppies	The Illuminati

MAN CRECHE

.com sign in or register

REVERSE BEER GOGGLES

If you are a member: Sign in.

View lager picture

Starting bid	£0.99	Place Bid >
End time:	14 mins 32 secs (30-May-07 13:40:20 BST)	
Postage costs:	£1.50 Royal Mail 2nd Class Standard Service to Worldwide	
Post to:	Worldwide	
Item location:	HERTFORDSHIRE, United Kingdom	
History:	0 bids	
You can also:	Watch This Item Get alerts via IM Email to a friend	

Meet the seller

Seller: Tomwaine74 (5)

Feedback: 100% Positive
Member: since 28-Dec-05 in United Kingdom
Registered as a private seller

Read feedback comments
Add to Favourite Sellers
View seller's other items

Ask seller a question

✉ Email the seller

Buy safely

1. Check the seller's reputation
   Score: 5 | 100% Positive
   Read feedback comments

Description

It's scientifically proven that the more you drink, the better looking members of the opposite sex become. Reverse beer goggles solve this problem by making members of the opposite sex appear to be marginally less attractive with each drink consumed, thus redressing the balance. They really do work!

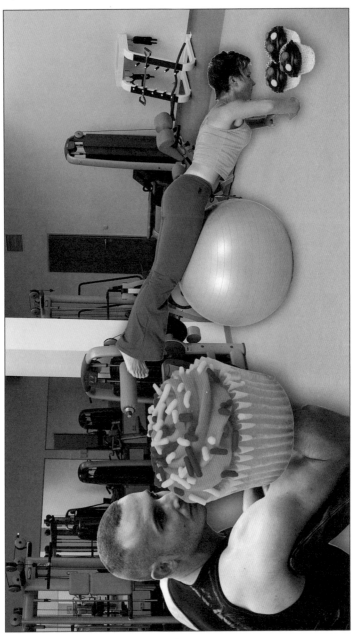

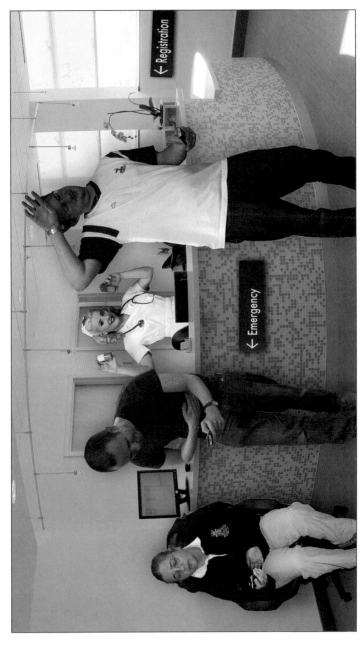

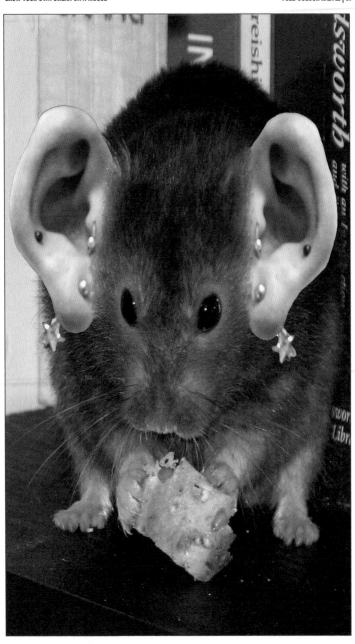

READERS' FUZZ

DO-IT-YOURSELF FUZZY LOGIC!

It was felt that for the last few pages it would be a good idea to give you some time to reflect on the fuzzy logic laid out for your consideration in this book. I also wanted to provide a blank canvas for your own blue-sky drinking exercises, so please go ahead and think outside your box, put pen to paper and unleash your own pub genius. If you are sitting on your own in the pub reading this, why not coax your fellow pub-goers into the creation of ideas?

The following pages have been laid out in the same format and categories used in my trusty beer-varnished notepad for pursuing the safe and humane capture of stray pub ideas. And if your local isn't particularly inspiring, feel free to design your own on pages 98 and 99.

Useful addresses for aspiring pub inventors.

Intellectual Property Office
(formerly the Patents Office)
Concept House
Cardiff Road
Newport
South Wales
NP10 8QQ
08459 500505
http://www.ipo.gov.uk

The British Inventors Society
http://www.thebis.org/index.php

The British Library (information on patents)
http://www.bl.uk/collections/patents/

Invention Europe (inventor's forum)
http://www.invention-europe.com/?newlang=eng

PUB IDEAS

Name of pub idea/invention . . . .
Name of pub where idea conceived . . . .
Date . . . .
Type of alcohol consumed . . . .
Amount of alcohol consumed . . . .
Names of co-conspirators . . . .

Technical drawing of idea

Written description of idea

Date/time the following day that I realized my idea was crap. . . . .

Name of pub idea/invention . . . .

Name of pub where idea conceived . . . .

Date . . . .

Type of alcohol consumed . . . .

Amount of alcohol consumed . . . .

Names of co-conspirators . . . .

Technical drawing of idea

Written description of idea

Date/time the following day that I realized my idea was crap. . . . .

Name of pub idea/invention . . . .

Name of pub where idea conceived . . . .

Date . . . .

Type of alcohol consumed . . . .

Amount of alcohol consumed . . . .

Names of co-conspirators . . . .

Technical drawing of idea

Written description of idea

Date/time the following day that I realized my idea was crap. . . . .

DESIGN YOUR IDEAL PUB

We all have visions of what our perfect pub would look like, so here's a chance to get some of the important details right. Break out the felt tips, flex that creativity and complete the pubs paraphernalia below.

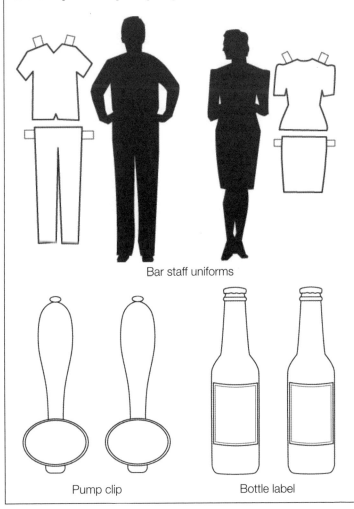

Bar staff uniforms

Pump clip

Bottle label

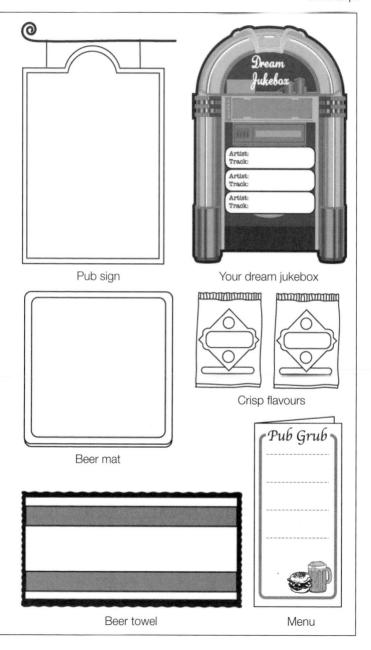

Pub sign

Your dream jukebox

Dream Jukebox

Artist:
Track:

Artist:
Track:

Artist:
Track:

Crisp flavours

Beer mat

Pub Grub

Beer towel

Menu

THINK TANKS

Here are some of the wonderful hostelries where the ideas in this book took flight. Thanks to the landlords and bar staff for not barring myself or any of the contributors of the book for talking our fuzzy logic in your pubs.

ANDOVER
Lamb Inn
21 Winchester Street,
SP10 2EA

Weyhill Fair
Weyhill, SP11 0PP

BIRMINGHAM
The Bull
1 Price Street, B4 6JU

Cap & Gown
458 Wilton Road, Aston, B6 6SN

BRIGHTON
Basketmakers Arms
12 Gloucester Road, BN1 4AD

Battle of Trafalgar
34 Guildford Road, BN1 3LW

Bugle Inn
24 St Martin's Street, BN2 3HJ

Dover Castle
43 Southover Street, BN2 9UE

Constant Service
(special mention, it was in this pub that the idea for the book came about)
96 Islingword Road, BN2 2SJ

CHELTENHAM & GLOUCESTER
Dick Whittington
100 Westgate Street, GL1 2PE

Royal Oak
43 The Burbage, Prestbury,
GL52 3DL

PADSTOW
Golden Lion Inn
Lanadwell Street, PL28 8AN

ST MAWGAN
Falcon Inn
TR8 4EP

HEREFORD
The Barrels
69 Owen Street, HR1 2JQ

LEEDS
Arcadia Ale & Wine Bar
34 Arndale Centre, Otley Road,
Headingley, LS6 2UE

Bricklayers Arms
8 Low Close Street,
Woodhouse, LS2 9EG

LEICESTER
The Globe
43 Silver Street, LE1 5EU

LONDON
BARNES
Red Lion
Castlenau, SW13 9RU

Tree House
73 White Hart Lane,
SW13 0PW

BATTERSEA
Prince Albert
85 Albert Bridge Road, SW11 4PF

CROYDON
Dog & Bull
24 Surrey Street, CR0 1RG

EAST LONDON
Pride of Spitalfields
3 Heneage Street, E1 5LJ

PARSONS GREEN
White Horse
1–3 Parsons Green, SW6 4UL

SOHO
Coach & Horses
5 Hill Street, W1J 5LD

BOROUGH
Market Porter
9 Stoney Street, SE1 9AA

WANDSWORTH
Freemasons
2 Northside, Wandsworth Common,
SW18 2SS

WIMBLEDON
Hand in Hand
6 Crooked Billet, SW19 4RQ

Nelson Arms
15 Merton High Street,
SW19 1DF

Fox and Grapes
9 Camp Road, SW19 4UN

MELTON MOWBRAY
Crown Inn
10 Burton Street, LE13 1AE

NOTTINGHAM
The Gatehouse
Toll House Hill, NG1 5FS

OVER WALLOP
White Hart
SO20 8HU

SAUCES OF INSPIRATION

The following beers have been scientifically proven to invoke pub ideas, thank you to these potent nectars and the breweries responsible.

Adnams Bitter – Adnams plc

Bishop's Finger – Shepherd Neame Brewery

Bitter & Twisted – Harviestoun Brewery Ltd

Black Sheep and Emmerdale Ale – Black Sheep Brewery

Bluebird Bitter – Coniston Brewing Co Ltd

Bombardier – Charles Wells Eagle Brewery

Boondoggle – Ringwood Brewery

Brains SA – SA Brain, The Cardiff Brewery

Brewers Gold – Crouch Vale Brewery

Budweiser Budvar – Budějovický Budvar

Cains Formidable Ale – Robert Cain & Co

Chimay – Abbaye de Notre-Dame

Cornish Knocker – Skinners

Double Chocolate Stout – Young's

Duvel – Brouwerij Moortgat

Black Dog – Elgood & Sons

ESB – Fuller's

Exmoor Gold – Exmoor Ales

Fursty Ferret – Hall & Woodhouse

Golden Champion – Hall & Woodhouse

Granny Wouldn't Like It – Wolf Brewery

Greene King IPA – Greene King

Guinness – Guinness Brewing

Hereford Pale Ale – Wye Valley Brewery

Hobgoblin – Wychwood Brewery

HSD – St Austell Brewery

Innis & Gunn Oak-aged Beer – Innis & Gunn Brewing Co

Leffe Triple – Brouwerij Hoegaarden

Liquid Lobotomy Stout – Garton Brewery

London Porter – Fuller's

London Pride – Fuller's

Nottingham Gold – Castle Rock Brewery

Old Hooky – Hook Norton Brewery

Old Mottled Cock – Leadmill Brewery

Old Peculier – Theakston

Old Thumper – Ringwood Brewery

Pauwel Kwak – Brouwerij Bosteels

RCH Ale Mary – RCH Brewery

Summer Lightning – Hop Back Brewery

Sunchaser – Everards Brewery

Sussex Best Bitter – Harvey's

Tanglefoot – Hall & Woodhouse

Thwaites Original – Daniel Thwaites plc

Wadworth 6X – Wadworth & Co

Winter Warmer – Young's

NAMED & SHAMED

I would like to take this opportunity to name some of the people who have contributed to this book; it wouldn't have been possible without their invaluable input of rubbish, ideas and beers.

Special thanks to:

Jo and Debbie @ CAMRA for not having me sectioned when I went to them with the proposal.

Simon @ CAMRA for his help with the final edits.

Mum and Dad and my two wonderful brothers/best mates (Angus and Duncan); again for not consulting the health authorities about the fragile state of my mental health.

Abi Lawrence-Jones for her priceless help and ideas.

Massive thanks to all of the following for their help and input of ideas:

Helen Mac, Fred, Grace, Ruth, Mark Thomas, Paul & Emma Phillips, Hayden, Simon Hutchings, Mark Smith (Smudge), Paul Minchin (Mach), Abi Mabey, Jenni Räikkönen, Chris Redmond, Andrew Robb, Claire Powell, James Harding (Panni), Paul Hickinbotham (Photos) Gareth Armstrong (Whatever model), Laura Frankland-Collick (Whatever model), Mark Stannard, Tasha, Renee, The Streatham Chiefs (sorry for missing training), Chloe Snape, Rich Hyams, Flavia Timiani, Arnaud Messager, Alex Bush, Cathy Norcott, My friends at The Sanctuary S-UK, Mary Liles, Disco, Adam Williams, Greg Taylor, Greg Hounsum, Arlanna Mazzi, Steve Olayton, Hoss Alexander, Haitham Rowley, Lanka, Jo & Danijela (for allowing me to write most of the book from their lovely tree house), Jim McDonagh, Steve Didd, Neil Donnell, Alex Bush, Monica Dalla Valle, Brian Copestick, Mr & Mrs Amit at the Nelson. Andy Cockell, Ghulam, Laetitia Wajnapel, Willie, The Lovells worldwide, Ted Waine (both), The Waines worldwide, Sady in the Cayman Islands, Neil Stephens, Mathew Baldwin, Arnie Arellano, Lide Murto, The Williams family – Debbie, Guy, Jake and Jess (some brilliant ideas), Emma Lloyd, Fen, Emily Britt, Mark Cumming, Karen West and little Gracey, The Jensen Bros, Sammy (Tuaca), Pete and Bianca, Cassie, Marie, Simmo, Tim O'Sullivan, Tom Stainer, Rachel Grant, Frank & Sabine Kleining, Denise Barnard, Momo Legall, Ronan Messager and Terry Robert.

CAMRA would like to thank the following people for 'volunteering' to act as models for the colour plates:

Cressida Feiler, Carwyn Davies, Gary Ranson, Gary Fowler, Kate Foster, Tom Stainer, Owen Morris, Guy Williams, Jake Williams and Mike Goring. Billy Bumbler appears courtesy of Emma Lloyd

And finally all the random punters who chipped in with their thoughts and ideas. Thank you all very much!

BOOKS FOR BEER LOVERS

CAMRA Books, the publishing arm of the Campaign for Real Ale, is the leading publisher of books on beer and pubs. Key titles include:

Good Beer Guide
Editor: ROGER PROTZ

The Good Beer Guide is the only guide you will need to find the right pint, in the right place, every time. It's the original and the best independent guide to around 4,500 pubs throughout the UK; in 2002 it was named as one of *The Guardian* newspaper's books of the year and *The Sun* newspaper rated the 2004 edition in the top 20 books of all time! This annual publication is a comprehensive and informative guide to the best real ale pubs in the UK, researched and written exclusively by CAMRA members and fully updated every year.

£14.99
ISBN 978 1 85249 231 1

The Book of Beer Knowledge
JEFF EVANS

A unique collection of entertaining trivia and essential wisdom, this is the perfect gift for beer lovers everywhere. Fully revised and updated it includes more than 200 entries covering the fictional 'celebrity landlords' of soap pubs, the harsh facts about the world's biggest brewers, bizarre beer names and the serious subject of fermentation.

£9.99
ISBN: 978 1 85249 198 7

300 Beers To Try Before You Die!
ROGER PROTZ

300 beers from around the world, hand-picked by award-winning journalist, author and broadcaster Roger Protz, to try before you die! A comprehensive, lavishly illustrated portfolio of top beers from the smallest micro-breweries in the United States to family-run British breweries and the world's largest brands. This book is indispensable for both beer novices and aficionados.

£14.99
ISBN 978 1 85249 213 7

Good Beer Guide Prague & The Czech Republic
EVAN RAIL

This fully updated and expanded version of a collectable classic is the first new edition to be produced by CAMRA for 10 years! It is the definitive guide for visitors to the Czech Republic and compulsory reading for fans of great beer, featuring more than 100 Czech breweries, 400 different beers and over 100 great places to try them. It includes listings of brewery-hotels and regional attractions for planning complete vacations outside of the capital, sections on historical background, how to get there and what to expect, as well as detailed descriptions of the 12 most common Czech beer styles.

£12.99
ISBN 13: 978 1 85249 233 5

Good Beer Guide Germany
STEVE THOMAS

The first ever comprehensive region-by-region guide to Germany's brewers, beer and outlets. Includes more than 1,200 breweries, 1,000 brewery taps and bars and more than 7,200 different beers. Complete with useful travel information on how to get there, informative essays on German beer and brewing plus beer festival listings.

£16.99
ISBN: 978 1 85248 219 9

Good Beer Guide Belgium
TIM WEBB

Now in its 5th edition and in full colour, this book has developed a cult following among committed beer lovers and beer tourists. It is the definitive, totally independent guide to understanding and finding the best of Belgian beer and an essential companion for any beer drinker visiting Belgium or seeking out Belgian beer in Britain. Includes details of the 120 breweries and over 800 beers in regular production, as well as 500 of the best hand-picked cafes in Belgium.

£12.99
ISBN: 978 1 85249 210 6

Beer Lover's Guide to Cricket
ROGER PROTZ

There are many books about cricket and many on beer, but this is the first book to bring the two subjects together. Leading beer writer and cricket enthusiast Roger Protz has visited the major grounds of all the First Class counties and gives in-depth profiles of them – their history, museums and memorabilia, plus listings of the best real ale pubs to visit within easy reach of each ground and details of the cask ales available. This fully illustrated book also features individual sections on the birth of the modern game of cricket and the history of each featured ground, making it an essential purchase for any cricket fan.

£16.99
ISBN: 978 1 85249 227 4

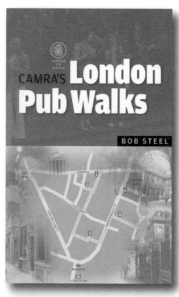

CAMRA's London Pub Walks
BOB STEEL

CAMRA's London Pub Walks enables you to explore the entire city while never being far away from a decent pint. A practical pocket-sized guide, it includes 30 walks around more than 180 pubs serving fine real ale, from the heart of the City and the bustling West End to majestic river-side routes and the leafy common of Wimbledon. The perfect companion for a day out discovering the real London.

£8.99
ISBN 978 1 85249 216 8

Beer, Bed & Breakfast
SUSAN NOWAK AND JILL ADAM

A unique and comprehensive guide to more than 500 of the UK's real ale pubs that also offer great accommodation, from tiny inns with a couple of rooms upstairs to luxury gastro pubs with country-house style bedrooms. All entries include contact details, type and extent of accommodation, beers served, meal types and times, and an easy-to-understand price guide to help plan your budget. This year, why not stay somewhere with a comfortable bed, a decent breakfast and a well-kept pint of beer, providing a home from home wherever you are in the country.

£14.99
ISBN: 978 1 85249 230 4

Order these and other CAMRA books online at **www.camra.org.uk/books**, ask at your local bookstore, or contact: CAMRA, 230 Hatfield Road, St Albans, AL1 4LW. Telephone **01727 867201**

IT TAKES ALL SORTS TO CAMPAIGN FOR REAL ALE

CAMRA, the Campaign for Real Ale, is an independent not-for-profit, volunteer-led consumer group. We actively campaign for full pints and more flexible licensing hours, as well as protecting the 'local' pub and lobbying government to champion pub-goers' rights.

CAMRA has more than 84,000 members from all ages and backgrounds, brought together by a common belief in the issues that CAMRA deals with and their love of good quality British beer. For just £20 a year, that's less than a pint a month, you can join CAMRA and enjoy the following benefits:

A monthly colour newspaper informing you about beer and pub news and detailing events and beer festivals around the country.

✳

Free or reduced entry to over 140 national, regional and local beer festivals.

✳

Money off many of our publications including the Good Beer Guide and the Good Bottled Beer Guide.

✳

Access to a members only section of our national website, **www.camra.org.uk**, which gives up-to-the-minute news stories and includes a special offer section with regular features saving money on beer and trips away.

✳

The opportunity to campaign to save pubs under threat of closure, for pubs to be open when people want to drink and a reduction in beer duty that will help Britain's brewing industry survive.

✳

Log onto **www.camra.org.uk** for
CAMRA membership information.

CAMPAIGN
FOR
REAL ALE

Do you feel passionately about your pint? Then why not join CAMRA

Just fill in the application form (or a photocopy of it) and the Direct Debit form on the next page to receive three months' membership FREE!

If you wish to join but do not want to pay by Direct Debit, fill in the application form below and send a cheque payable to CAMRA to: CAMRA, 230 Hatfield Road, St Albans, Hertfordshire, AL1 4LW. Please note that non Direct Debit payments will incur a £2 surcharge. Figures are given below.

Current rate	Direct Debit	Non DD
☐ Single Membership (UK & EU)	£20	£22
☐ Concessionary Membership (under 26 or 60 and over)	£11	£13
☐ Joint Membership	£25	£27
☐ Concessionary Joint Membership	£14	£16

Life membership information is available on request.

Title _____ Surname _____

Forename(s) _____

Address _____

_____

Postcode _____ Date of Birth _____

Email address _____

Signature _____

Partner's details if required

Title _____ Surname _____

Forename(s) _____

Date of Birth _____

Email address _____

Please tick here ☐ if you would like to receive occasional emails from CAMRA (at no point will your details be released to a third party).

Find out more about CAMRA at **www.camra.org.uk**

Instruction to your Bank or Building Society to pay by Direct Debit

Please fill in the form and send to: Campaign for Real Ale Ltd. 230 Hatfield Road, St. Albans, Herts. AL1 4LW

Name and full postal address of your Bank or Building Society

To The Manager _____ Bank or Building Society

Address

Postcode

Name (s) of Account Holder (s)

Bank or Building Society account number

Branch Sort Code

Reference Number

Banks and Building Societies may not accept Direct Debit instructions for some types of account

Originator's Identification Number

9	2	6	1	2	9

FOR CAMRA OFFICIAL USE ONLY
This is not part of the instruction to your Bank or Building Society

Membership Number

Name

Postcode

Instruction to your Bank or Building Society

Please pay CAMRA Direct Debits from the account detailed on this instruction subject to the safeguards assured by the Direct Debit Guarantee. I understand that this instruction may remain with CAMRA and, if so, will be passed electronically to my Bank/Building Society

Signature(s)

Date

✂ detached and retained this section

This Guarantee should be detached and retained by the payer.

The Direct Debit Guarantee

- This Guarantee is offered by all Banks and Building Societies that take part in the Direct Debit Scheme. The efficiency and security of the Scheme is monitored and protected by your own Bank or Building Society.

- If the amounts to be paid or the payment dates change CAMRA will notify you 10 working days in advance of your account being debited or as otherwise agreed.

- If an error is made by CAMRA or your Bank or Building Society, you are guaranteed a full and immediate refund from your branch of the amount paid.

- You can cancel a Direct Debit at any time by writing to your Bank or Building Society. Please also send a copy of your letter to us.

Russell Mabey (1970 - 2007)

So go well, friend, brother, son, father, lover.
And take with you the love of ten thousand hearts
The fires you lit in each of them
Will burn eternally
And the smoke will be beautiful
We will meet there in dreams
Until we fly together again.

Written by Chris Redmond - January 2007